Virtual Tax

Virtual Tax: The Taxation of Cryptocurrency

Published by Desert Mystery Publishing

2023 edition published January 2023

ISBN: 979-8-9870872-0-6

Cover art by Mariah Wall
Book layout by Paper Crane Books

Virtual Tax:
The taxation of cryptocurrency

2023 Edition

by Amy M. Wall, EA, MBA

*For Gary Payne, uncomplaining (mostly)
and patient husband*

Important Notice:

Tax law as it pertains to virtual currency is very much in its infancy. This book is designed to provide information on the taxation of virtual currency — to the best of the author's understanding — as of the date of publication. Future guidance from the IRS is needed to clarify many issues.

For these reasons, the author and publisher do not guarantee or warrant any information contained herein: competent professional advice should always be sought for your particular situation.

Further, the author and publisher are not engaged in legal services, and no information contained herein should be construed as legal advice. As an IRS Circular 230 practitioner, I have no responsibility for any positions you take on your tax return, unless I have prepared and signed that tax return. For detailed analysis of your tax situation, please consult your tax advisor.

Table of Contents

PART I
INTRODUCTION TO VIRTUAL CURRENCY

PART II

PART III
THE IRS' REIGN OF TERROR

PART IV
APPLYING THE RULES AND REGS

PART V
UPCOMING LEGISLATION

PART VI
TAX MATTERS

Preface

THIS EDITION OF VIRTUAL TAX includes background on virtual currency that can help tax professionals get more comfortable dealing with this subject. If you're already a miner, trader, etc., feel free to skip the first part of this book. You probably know more than I do.

From a tax standpoint, the difficulty presented by virtual currency is simply this: it's often used as a currency, and is even called currency, but it's taxed as property. Because it is taxed as property, there are taxable gains and losses upon sale or trade, or upon receiving it as compensation. Because it is also used as currency, purchases and sales occur frequently and often in micro amounts. This is a new type of asset that all of us in Tax World are struggling to get our (virtual) arms around. I was truly hoping to not publish an update to this book until 2024 — continuing my practice of updating every other year — but there's been so much new activity in the Cryptoverse that waiting isn't an option.

Part I

INTRODUCTION TO VIRTUAL CURRENCY

1

Virtual Currency — Why It's a Thing

FIRST, LET'S UNDERSTAND THAT THERE are indeed differences between digital currency, virtual currency, and cryptocurrency.

If you Google these terms, you'll find different definitions presented by different people but, basically, digital currency is just what you think it is: currency that is stored and transferred electronically. Most money in the world is digital currency. Your debit card could be considered digital. For that matter, your bank account is probably digital as well. Your bank certainly doesn't have all its customers' money sitting in a vault onsite.

Virtual currency is a type of digital currency that is controlled by its creators and may be used for payment among members of a particular virtual community. This type of currency has no central point of regulation — no bank, no credit card agency, no broker — and, though it may be used by natural or legal persons as a means of exchange, virtual currency does not possess the status of legal tender; it is not a fiat currency in the United States.

Cryptocurrency is a subset of virtual currency; it refers to a type of virtual currency that utilizes encryption algorithms and techniques to ensure security. Bitcoin, Ether, Litecoin, etc., are cryptocurrencies.

The IRS uses the terms "virtual currency," "cryptocurrency," and "digital assets" apparently without distinction, so I use those terms interchangeably as well.

Also note that all the concepts in this book apply equally to coins and tokens; the IRS makes no distinction between the two when it comes to taxes.

People who aren't familiar with virtual currency often ask, "What problems are virtual and cryptocurrencies trying to solve? Why is this even a thing?"

It's a thing because many people see that virtual currency has the potential to solve a significant money problem.

Money has always had its problems. Back in the bartering days, the problem was finding someone who had something you wanted and also wanted something that you had. If I had lots of strawberries but no bread, then my goal would be to find someone who had lots of bread, but no strawberries. Clearly not an efficient system.

Then there were some goods that were fairly easily traded without requiring direct barter: salt, animal skins, weapons, etc. The problem at that point was one of transportation and storage, as these items took up physical space and had to be moved from place to place.

There were some early currencies in the form of metal coins. The first minted currency was that of a country called Lydia (an Iron Age kingdom in the area of Turkey) in 600 BC. These coins were a mixture of silver and gold and were minted in different denominations.

The Chinese then took it to the next level with paper money during the Tang Dynasty. Interesting tidbit: American bills say, "In God We Trust"; the Chinese bill said, "All counterfeiters will be decapitated." Serious stuff.

The first paper currency used in Europe was printed in Sweden in 1601. The first paper money in America was issued by the Massachusetts Bay Colony in 1690 to finance a military expedition to Canada.

Paper money was distrusted for a long time (much as virtual currency is distrusted now); the gold standard helped citizens overcome that distrust. The gold standard meant that the government would redeem paper money for its value in gold. The Federal Reserve was created in 1913 to stabilize gold and currency values. By 1970, the US no longer held enough gold to cover all the dollar holdings in the world; President Nixon took the US off the gold standard in August of 1971.

As of that time, money's value became *perceived*, rather than *actual*; money became a *concept*, rather than a *thing*.

The problem with paper or metal currencies is, again, transportation. How do I pay someone who isn't sitting in front of me?

Thus, credit cards. Credit cards originated with Diners Club in 1950 and were used mainly for travel and entertainment. American Express was launched in 1958 and introduced the first plastic (rather than paper) card. From there, we've gone to mobile payment systems.

We no longer have a problem with paying long distance; instead, we have another problem. If you want to pay someone who isn't sitting in front of you holding their hand out for cash, you need a third party. Every time. EVERY. TIME. You need a bank to process the debit card transaction. Or you need a credit card processor to handle the credit card payment. Or you need Paypal. Or Zelle.

In fact, there's literally no way to pay someone who isn't sitting in front of you with their hand out unless you have a third party facilitating the transaction. And this wouldn't be much of a problem, except that this third party has to be paid for their services.

Can you imagine how much money is poured into the waiting hands of banks, credit card processors, etc.? I recently saw an estimate of $42.4 billion dollars collected from vendors by credit card companies in 2016. That's BILLIONS of dollars.

So — goes the thinking — what if we could do without that third party? What if there was a way to process payments that didn't involve cash and didn't involve third parties sucking up billions of dollars? And what if people who didn't have access to banks (or couldn't afford the fees) could send and receive currency? Wouldn't that be a good thing?

This idea is called "decentralizing"...and thus, virtual currency was born.

In November 1998 a computer engineer named Wei Dai published an essay proposing an anonymous, distributed electronic cash system called B-money.

In 2005, a computer scientist and cryptographer named Nick Szabo proposed a decentralized financial system incorporating time stamped blocks and proof-of-work strings; the result would be secure storage and transferring. He called it "Bit Gold."

In 2009, an unknown person or persons named Nakamoto authored a paper on Bitcoin and devised the first blockchain database. Bitcoin is a decentralized currency (so no bank or credit card processing agencies). It utilizes a distributed ledger, meaning that the "books", as it were, are open and available to anyone on the system. (Understand here that the names of users aren't on the ledger; what is seen is just the relevant information about the transaction such as the amount, date, etc.)

With a distributed ledger all transaction histories are stored and updated continuously, constantly, reliably. The data relevant to each transaction is stored in a data string called a "blockchain", which is completely secure and unalterable.

The idea of a secure data string has many possibilities outside the creation of virtual currency. The blockchain is considered by many people to be the biggest modern revolution since the internet.

The first Bitcoin transaction, now famous, occurred in 2010 when programmer Laszlo Hanyecz purchased two Papa John's pizzas for 10,000 BTC (Bitcoins).

Since that time, thousands of "altcoins" (coins other than Bitcoin) have been created. For tax purposes, you don't need to know much about them, other than that they exist.

2

Concepts

THIS CHAPTER IS INTENDED AS an overview of some basic concepts underlying cryptocurrencies. You can Google any of this stuff; I'm just trying to save you the trouble. They are in alphabetical order, as it was impossible to determine which were very important, as opposed to just sort of important or not very important. They're all important in one way or another.

Please note that this is in no way an exhaustive list; the Cryptoverse is constantly evolving, and new ideas and projects are being developed every day.

Address: A string of letters and numbers representing a place where crypto can be sent to and from, like a bank account number.

Airdrop: An airdrop is a marketing campaign that distributes coins or tokens to a hot wallet, in the hopes of getting people to use them.

Altcoin: An altcoin is simply anything that isn't Bitcoin. Altcoins can be very popular and valuable (like Ethereum) or they can be unknown and worth basically nothing.

Baking: The process by which new transaction block are added to the Tezos chain, similar to mining and staking.

Bitcoin: Bitcoin was the very first decentralized digital currency, launched on January 3, 2009, utilizing cryptographic programming and blockchain technology. The currency was created by some unknown person or persons calling themselves Satoshi Nakamoto. To this day, no one knows who Satoshi Nakamoto is or was. Bitcoin is unlike many other cryptocurrencies in that it has what's called a "hard cap," meaning that the number of coins that can ever exist is limited. The limit is 21 million. If you own one full Bitcoin, you automatically become a member of the "Twenty-One Million" club. There are t-shirts you can buy. (Not kidding about that.)

Block: A block is a chunk of data in a blockchain. The block is a transaction record of coins being transferred from one person or account to another person or account. Each block holds a certain amount of data; once that limit is reached, a new block is created.

Blockchain: Blockchain technology has been called the greatest invention since the internet. A blockchain is a series of blocks (see "Block" above). The chain gets longer and longer as time goes on and more transactions are made, but no block can ever be altered. Once a transaction is recorded on the blockchain, it's there for eternity.

Central Bank Digital Currency (CBDC): These are digital currencies issued by a central bank which may then become fiat currency for that country.

Cryptocurrency: This is a subset of digital currency. There are literally thousands of cryptocurrencies in existence at this time; some of the better-known ones are Ethereum, Litecoin, and Ripple. They each have a 3-letter acronym, much like the way stocks have a ticker symbol. Sometimes they're easy to figure out — BTC is Bitcoin, ETH is Ethereum. Sometimes they're harder — XRP is Ripple.

Cryptography: The word "crypto" means secret or hidden. Try not to associate it with the word "crypt," but you probably can't help yourself. Cryptography is the type of programming used by cryptocurrencies so that only the sender and the receiver can decode it. Other people can't break into it. This type of programming has been literally decades in the making.

DApps: These are applications designed to carry out actions without a third-party intermediary. These applications are usually built on the Ethereum blockchain.

Decentralization: This is a very important idea. Decentralization means that there's no third party involved. Our current financial system relies heavily on third parties (banks, credit card agencies, etc.) to keep the system going. Cryptocurrencies, in the ideal world, don't require third parties in order to function. Note that as of now, this isn't the case. Most of us get our cryptocurrencies on an exchange of some sort, and those exchanges do indeed charge fees. The idea (maybe "the hope" is more accurate) is that eventually everyone would get paid in crypto and thus have crypto to spend without having to get it on an exchange.

Decentralized Exchange (DEX): This is a peer-to-peer exchange that allows users to trade currencies without an intermediary.

Distributed Ledger: Distributed ledgers are ledgers in which data is stored across a network of decentralized nodes.

Exchanges: Just as you buy stocks from a stockbroker, you buy cryptocurrencies through an exchange. Many crypto owners store their cryptocurrencies directly on the exchange, such as Coinbase. The risk here is that if the exchange is hacked, your cryptocurrency is gone. The blockchain is completely secure; exchanges aren't.

Faucet: This is a cryptocurrency reward system, generally on a website or app, that rewards users for completing small tasks.

Fiat currency: Legal tender backed by a central government. Fiat currency in the U.S. is the dollar.

FOMO: A type of buying behavior that has brought most investors into cryptocurrency. It stands for "Fear of Missing Out." (And then there's JOMO, which is "Joy of Missing Out.")

Fork: Programming changes create hart and soft forks in blockchains. A hard fork may create a new currency.

Gas: Gas is a fee that developers and users have to pay to the Ethereum network. Gas is paid in Ether, and since that ETH is being traded for a service, the paying of gas is a taxable event.

Genesis block: The first block of any cryptocurrency to be mined.

Governance token: This is a token that allows holder to vote on decisions in an ecosystem.

Halving: Halving is a feature written into the Bitcoin code that divides the number of new coins being mined in half, approximately every four years. The idea is to not have all the 21 million coins released into circulation too quickly.

Hard cap: The absolute max amount of any supply of a digital asset.

HODL: This phrase was actually first seen as a typo on a Bitcoin forum in 2013; he meant to say "hold." Since then, some people use the phrase to mean "hold on for dear life." Either way, a HODLER is someone who's holding on for the long term.

Initial Coin Offering (ICO): This is a sort of IPO in the crypto world. An ICO, IDO, IEO or ITO are all ways of raising funds for a new service, coin or token to the world.

Keys: Cryptocurrencies are owned via the possession of two "keys," a private key and a public key. The public key is your wallet's address, similar to a bank account number. This can be shared with others, as it's this key that allows people to send crypto to you. The private key, on the other hand, is an encrypted code that allows direct access to the currencies. Owning the private key equals owning the crypto. If your private keys are lost or stolen, your crypto is gone.

Liquidity pool: Crypto assets kept by exchanges to allow the trading of cryptocurrencies. Allowing your currency to be held in a liquidity pool is called liquidity mining.

Market Capitalization: This is the total value of all coins that have been mined or staked. It's calculated by multiplying the number of coins in the world by the current value of the coins.

Mining/Staking: Each type of cryptocurrency has a different way of validating transactions and allowing new data block to be created. Some currencies, such as Bitcoin, are "mined." Others, such as Ethereum, are staked. From a tax standpoint, though, it's all the same thing.

Mining pool: A number of miners pooling resources to increase the odds of winning mining rewards. There are also staking pools for currencies that are staked rather than mined.

Mining rewards: The crypto received by miners for finding and validating a data block.

NFTs: Non-fungible tokens are data strings that represent the ownership of digital assets like art, music, memes, music, collectibles, and so on. They're usually built on the Ethereum blockchain.

Peer-to-Peer or P2P: A transaction involving two users but no third party. This is how cryptocurrencies hope to be used.

Pump and dump scheme: Fraudulent activity involving the artificial inflation of a crypto's price through making false or misleading statements.

Rug pull: A scam involving developers who start a project, market it, then take investor's money and vanish.

Smart Contract: This is an algorithmic program that automatically executes the terms of a contract without the involvement of a third-party. Smart contracts are generally built on the Ethereum blockchain.

Stablecoin: A stablecoin attempts to peg its value to a non-digital asset. Some are pegged to the U.S. dollar, others to precious metals. It's not unheard of for the sta-blecoin to "lose its peg" and dip below that value.

Token: This term is most typically sued to refer to a cryp-toasset such as Chainlink or Aave, that runs on another cryptocurrency's blockchain.

Utility token: Tokens designed for product or service use, rather than a currency.

Wallet: Just as coins and paper bills go into a physical wallet, cryptocurrencies are stored in another kind of wallet. "Hot" wallets are connected to the internet; "cold" wallets aren't. Hot wallets are generally more convenient for users, but they're more susceptible to hacking. Mobile wallets are crypto wallet stored on a cell phone. What's actually IN the wallets? The keys to the cryptocurrencies (see "Keys" above). Some cryptocurrency owners simply write the keys down on a piece of paper; others actually memorize the keys. (I know, what could go wrong?!)

Whale: An investor who has enough cryptocurrency to actually be able to manipulate the market.

Yield farming: Earning interest by investing crypto in decentralized markets.

Part II

1

GAO Report of May 2013

ISSUES CONCERNING THE TAXATION OF virtual currency were first addressed in May of 2013 by the United States Government Accountability Office in a report to the Committee on Finance, U.S. Senate. It was called "Virtual Economies and Currencies: Additional IRS Guidance Could Reduce Tax Compliance Risks."

It's enjoyable reading, particularly since the Report is far more interested in MMORPGs (Massively Multiplayer Online Role-Playing Games) than in Bitcoin. I discuss the tax implications of MMORPGs in Part IV, Chapter 16.

The Report defined virtual currency as "... generally, a digital unit of exchange that is not backed by a government-issued legal tender. Virtual currencies can be used entirely within a virtual economy or can be used in lieu of a government-issued currency to purchase goods and services in the real economy." I guess that's as good a definition as any.

The Report laid out a case for taxable transactions

resulting from the use of virtual currency in or out of the context of virtual economies such as MMORPGs. It stated that there are tax compliance risks involved with virtual currency and virtual economics, specifically taxpayers' lack of knowledge about the tax requirements; uncertainty over how to characterize income; uncertainty over how to calculate basis (more detail on that later) for gains; challenges with third-party reporting (the lack thereof); and tax evasion.

Bottom line? Taxpayers don't know how to report their virtual currency income, and might not want to, even if they did know how. (Which sounds pretty much like the so-called real economy, come to think of it.) Further, as the use of virtual currencies and virtual economies grows, the risk of tax noncompliance grows as well.

The Report acknowledged that back in 2007 the IRS had identified and surveyed various information sources relative to virtual economics but had ultimately decided that the amount of lost revenue did not justify taking resources away from higher priority needs. Finally, the Report called the IRS out for not having issued guidance specific to virtual currencies outside of virtual economies and suggested that the IRS find relatively low-cost ways to provide information to taxpayers.

2

Taxpayer Advocate Service Report 2013

THIS REPORT WAS ONE OF the things that helped get
the IRS off the couch and actually issue some guidance
for cryptocurrency. Prior to 2013, the IRS had actually
put up a page on the internet stating that cryptocurrency
wasn't worth their time. That page is long gone.

Taxpayer Advocate Service Report, MSP #24

DIGITAL CURRENCY: The IRS Should Issue
Guidance to Assist Users of Digital Currency

RESPONSIBLE OFFICIALS

William J. Wilkins, Chief Counsel

Karen Schiller, Commissioner, Small Business/
Self-Employed Division

Debra Holland, Commissioner, Wage and Investment Division

Heather C. Maloy, Commissioner, Large Business and International Division

DEFINITION OF PROBLEM

The use of digital currencies, such as bitcoin, is growing. In the four months between July and December 2013, bitcoin usage has increased by over 75 percent — from about 1,700 transactions per hour to over 3,000. Over the same period, the market value of bitcoins in circulation increased more than ten-fold from about $1.1 billion to $12.6 billion. Over 10,000 businesses reportedly accept payment in bitcoins.

The IRS has not issued specific guidance addressing the tax treatment or reporting requirements applicable to digital currency transactions. Differing opinions are available on the Internet. People who are trying to comply with their federal income tax reporting obligations have complained that they are unsure about the rules. Thus, IRS-issued guidance would promote tax compliance, particularly among those who want to comply. Moreover, it would eliminate the ambiguity that may encourage some digital currency users to avoid taxation and information reporting.

ANALYSIS OF PROBLEM

Digital currency is different from government-backed currency.

Unlike the U.S. dollar, a digital currency does not rely on a banking network for payment processing and is not backed or controlled by a government. Bitcoin is an example of a digital currency.

Bitcoin relies on cryptography and a peer-to-peer network to process and verify payments. People can purchase bitcoins on an exchange or "mine" a limited amount by solving cryptographic problems — an activity that facilitates commerce by verifying or clearing transactions in the public ledger (called a "block chain"). If a customer wants to send bitcoins to a merchant, the merchant gives the customer a public key. The customer completes the transaction by signing with his or her public and private keys.

Digital currency is not subject to government manipulation, and facilitates quick, anonymous, irreversible, low-cost transactions.

Bitcoin appeals to those who do not trust banks or other financial institutions, who want to make quick, irrevocable transfers without paying for currency conversion, or who value privacy. The supply of bitcoins is limited and controlled by an algorithm. Unlike government-backed currency, no central authority can devalue bitcoins by printing more. Created in 2009, the supply of bitcoins will gradually increase, as they are minted (i.e., "mined") at a controlled rate, until approximately 2140 when about 21 million are in circulation. Thus, it is less likely to lose value as a result of government intervention or mismanagement than a government-backed currency. Indeed, turmoil in Cyprus reportedly led to a sharp increase in the price of bitcoins as people sought refuge in the digital currency as a kind of cyber gold.

Bitcoin promotes anonymity because it uses peer-to-peer technology to operate with no central authority or clearinghouse. Although every transaction is open to the public, the identity of the parties is not. A person's bitcoins exist only on his or her computer, rather than on a centralized server that could be monitored and linked to an identity.

Bitcoin is also convenient. International buyers and sellers can conduct transactions without the expense of having an intermediary clear them or convert funds into a national currency. Certain automated teller machines (ATMs), which went on sale in 2013, can convert between dollars and bitcoins, and bitcoins can be spent via computer or mobile phone.

Among the potential benefits to merchants of bitcoin transactions are that they usually clear relatively quickly, are irreversible, carry low processing fees, and may avoid information reporting. By comparison, credit card transactions generally take longer to clear, can be reversed, and are frequently subject to higher fees and greater information reporting.

Bitcoin is growing.

As noted above, in the five months between July and December 2013, bitcoin usage has increased by over 75 percent — from about 1,700 transactions per hour to over 3,000.16 Over the same period, the market value of bitcoins in circulation increased more than ten-fold from about $1.1 billion to $12.6 billion. Traders at major banks reportedly keep watch on the bitcoin exchange rate. Over 10,000 businesses reportedly accept payment in bitcoins. BitPay, a business that helps merchants accept bitcoins, reports that over 10,000 businesses accept them. About 60 percent of its clients are in the United States.

Recent developments could increase bitcoin acceptance. The World Wide Web Consortium (W3C), a web browser standard-setting body, recently took steps that will allow most browsers to recognize bitcoin payment links. For example, a website could have a "purchase with bitcoin" button, making it easier for consumers to use bitcoins for Internet purchases.

In addition, pending sales tax legislation could increase the use of bitcoins. Several bills would allow states to require out of state vendors to collect sales tax on sales to in-state residents. These bills only provide for sales tax collection when the seller knows the purchaser's address. Unlike credit card sales that transmit the

customer's billing address, a bitcoin sale does not identify the residence of the buyer, potentially allowing
purchasers to avoid sales tax if they use bitcoins to pay
for property that does not require a shipping address
(e.g., software or music). For all of these reasons, bitcoins
could become more popular as a result of this legislation.

Moreover, if digital currency establishes itself as
a new asset class that is not correlated with other asset
classes, then investors who want a diversified portfolio
may begin to purchase it as an investment rather than
as a medium of exchange. Thus, the use of bitcoin and
similar digital currencies is likely to increase.

Taxpayers want to know the tax consequences of digital currency transactions.

Legitimate businesses — those who want to comply
with the rules and do not want to be associated with
tax evaders or criminal enterprises — have urged the
government to issue clear rules about the tax consequences of digital currency transactions. Following
a 2008 recommendation by the National Taxpayer
Advocate to issue guidance on the tax treatment of the
transfer of digital items and currency, the IRS created a
web page that says it has already "provided guidance on
the tax treatment of bartering, gambling, business and
hobby income — issues that are similar to activities in
online gaming worlds." It suggests that existing guidance
covers digital currency transactions, but does not explain

when these transactions are sufficiently analogous to the transactions described in the guidance to be covered by existing rules.

To fill the void left by the IRS's lack of specific guidance, interested parties are posting answers to "frequently asked questions" on the Internet about the tax treatment of digital currency transactions, some of which may be incorrect, incomplete, or misleading. For example, a popular tax preparation company's blog describes bitcoin as "The Taxless Currency." Scholarly papers and at least one digital book are also available on the subject. These materials often raise more questions than they answer.

For example, a U.S. resident generally does not recognize gain or loss when using dollars to purchase goods and services. As a result, some people may be surprised to learn that using bitcoins to purchase goods or services could trigger taxable gains or losses on the bitcoins themselves. Moreover, the character of any such gains or losses is not readily apparent. If a bitcoin is deemed property, then spending it could produce capital gains or losses. On the other hand, if a bitcoin is a "nonfunctional currency" for tax purposes, then spending it could produce ordinary income or loss under Internal Revenue Code (IRC) § 988(a)(1).

Transactions involving digital currency may trigger information reporting, but the IRS is unlikely to get many reports unless it explains the rules.

U.S. citizens and residents who hold more than $10,000 in foreign accounts are required to report the accounts on Form 114, Report of Foreign Bank and Financial Accounts (FBAR). Those with certain foreign financial assets in excess of $50,000 must also report foreign accounts (and certain other foreign financial asset information) on Form 8938, Statement of Specified Foreign Financial Assets. Like cash, bitcoins that are not held in an "account" may not be subject to these reporting requirements. However, some have speculated about whether bitcoins in e-wallets located on servers in foreign countries should be reported on these forms. Moreover, when a business receives more than $10,000 in cash, it is generally required to report the transaction on Form 8300, Report of Cash Payments Over $10,000 Received in a Trade or Business, but it is not clear that the receipt of $10,000 in bitcoins would trigger this reporting requirement.

In addition, bitcoin transactions are not necessarily subject to the information reporting that applies to credit cards and other payment cards under IRC § 6050W. Under this provision, a "payment settlement entity" is required to report the amount paid to those who receive more than 200 payments, provided they receive more than $20,000 in total. A payment settlement entity generally must have a contractual obligation to make a payment in settlement of a transaction. However, bitcoin transactions use a peer-to-peer network that does not depend on a contractual settlement mechanism. For this reason, it is not clear that they would trigger a reporting requirement. Thus, it would be helpful for the government to provide examples illustrating the extent to which each of these reporting regimes apply to common digital currency transactions.

CONCLUSION

It is the government's responsibility to inform the public about the rules they are required to follow. The lack of clear answers to basic questions such as when and how taxpayers should report gains and losses on digital currency transactions probably encourages tax avoidance.

Many law-abiding taxpayers want to comply and to distinguish themselves from tax evaders. Some are frustrated by the IRS's lack of guidance. According to the summary of a book that purports to identify bitcoin-related tax issues:

> The IRS is famous for expecting people to comply with tax rules that aren't even written yet. And, they have given no indication that they are going to help Bitcoin users out any time soon....

Because Bitcoin is new technology and not easily defined, in a legal sense, this will allow you to be much more creative and flexible and legally reduce your tax liability.

Promulgating guidance would make it more difficult for taxpayers to be "creative," allow law-abiding taxpayers to keep up with the times without undue burden, reduce traps for the unwary, and make it easier for IRS employees to enforce the law.

RECOMMENDATIONS

The IRS has not explained how existing rules apply to digital currency transactions with enough specificity to allow taxpayers to be sure they are following them or for IRS employees to enforce them. The National Taxpayer Advocate recommends that the IRS issue guidance that at least answers the following questions:

1. When will receiving or using digital currency trigger gains and losses?

2. When will these gains and losses be taxed as ordinary income or capital gains?

3. What information reporting, withholding, backup withholding, and recordkeeping

requirements apply to digital currency transactions?

4. When should digital currency holdings be reported on an FBAR or Form 8938, *Statement of Specified Foreign Financial Assets*?

By the way, that last item? When to report digital currency holding on Form 8938? Here we are, practically a decade later, and the IRS still hasn't answered the question. Someone should be embarrassed, and it isn't the taxpayer.

3
Notice 2014-21

THE IRS RESPONDED A YEAR later, on March 15, 2014, by issuing a whopping, no-expense-spared, six pages of guidance in the form of Notice 2014-21. A Notice is usually issued prior to being officially published in the Internal Revenue Bulletin; the Bulletin is the ultimate authority, and the Notice is simply a preview of what's going into the Internal Revenue Bulletin. So yes, the Notice is official IRS guidance.

Let's read through the Notice together to make sure we understand the important points. The text of the Notice is quoted verbatim and is indented; my comments are shown in bold type.

SECTION 1. PURPOSE

This notice describes how existing general tax principles apply to transactions using virtual currency. The notice provides this guidance in the form of answers to frequently asked questions.

SECTION 2. BACKGROUND

The Internal Revenue Service (IRS) is aware that "virtual currency" may be used to pay for goods or services, or held for investment. Virtual currency is a digital representation of value that functions as a medium of exchange, a unit of account, and/or a store of value. In some environments, it operates like "real" currency — i.e., the coin and paper money of the United States or of any other country that is designated as legal tender, circulates, and is customarily used and accepted as a medium of exchange in the country of issuance — but it does not have legal tender status in any jurisdiction.

Virtual currency that has an equivalent value in real currency, or that acts as a substitute for real currency, is referred to as "convertible" virtual currency. Bitcoin is one example of a convertible virtual currency. Bitcoin can be digitally traded between users and can be purchased for, or exchanged into, U.S. dollars, Euros, and other real or virtual currencies. For a more comprehensive description of convertible virtual currencies to date, see Financial Crimes Enforcement Network

(FinCEN) *Guidance on the Application of FinCEN's Regulations to Persons Administering, Exchanging, or Using Virtual Currencies* (FIN-2013-G001, March 18, 2013).

SECTION 3. SCOPE

In general, the sale or exchange of convertible virtual currency, or the use of convertible virtual currency to pay for goods or services in a real-world economy transaction, has tax consequences that may result in a tax liability. This notice addresses only the U.S. federal tax consequences of transactions in, or transactions that use, convertible virtual currency, and the term "virtual currency" as used in Section 4 refers only to convertible virtual currency.

No inference should be drawn with respect to virtual currencies not described in this notice. The Treasury Department and the IRS recognize that there may be other questions regarding the tax consequences of virtual currency not addressed in this notice that warrant consideration. Therefore, the Treasury Department and the IRS request comments from the public regarding other types or aspects of virtual currency transactions that should be addressed in future guidance.

For purposes of the FAQs in this notice, the taxpayer's functional currency is assumed to be the U.S. dollar, the taxpayer is assumed to use the cash receipts and disbursements method of accounting and the taxpayer is assumed not to be under common control with any other party to a transaction.

OK, so far, so good. The IRS recognizes the existence of virtual currency, and that it may be used to purchase "real world" goods and services. The Notice makes an important distinction between convertible virtual currencies (meaning currencies that may be utilized in place of fiat currency) as opposed to a virtual currency that may not be so utilized.

SECTION 4. FREQUENTLY ASKED QUESTIONS

Q-1: How is virtual currency treated for federal tax purposes?

A-1: For federal tax purposes, virtual currency is treated as property. General tax principles applicable to property transactions apply to transactions using virtual currency.

This is the single most important statement in the Notice. For the tax-savvy, all the rest of this Notice is just commentary. Defining virtual currency as property means that every time virtual currency is spent, sold, traded, exchanged, gifted, donated, inherited, or even lost, a potential taxable event has taken place. For virtual currency users, defining virtual currency as property was a devastating blow.

> **Q-2:** Is virtual currency treated as currency for purposes of determining whether a transaction results in foreign currency gain or loss under U.S. federal tax laws?
>
> **A-2:** No. Under currently applicable law, virtual currency is not treated as currency that could generate foreign currency gain or loss for U.S. federal tax purposes.

More bad news. Foreign currency gain has a de minimis of $200, meaning that if you have a gain of less than $200 you don't have to bother reporting it. No such luck with virtual currency.

Q-3: Must a taxpayer who receives virtual currency as payment for goods or services include in computing gross income the fair market value of the virtual currency?

A-3: Yes. A taxpayer who receives virtual currency as payment for goods or services must, in computing gross income, include the fair market value of the virtual currency, measured in U.S. dollars, as of the date that the virtual currency was received. See Publication 525, Taxable and Nontaxable Income, for more information on miscellaneous income from exchanges involving property or services.

This was obvious as soon as the Notice said the word "property." Of course, anytime you receive property in exchange for goods and services, you have income. Out in the "real" world, this is called barter income: I'll do your bookkeeping in exchange for you painting my house. Both sides have reportable income which, as dutiful US citizens, they have reported on their tax returns.

Q-4: What is the basis of virtual currency received as payment for goods or services in Q&A-3?

A-4: The basis of virtual currency that a tax-payer receives as payment for goods or services in Q&A-3 is the fair market value of the virtual currency in U.S. dollars as of the date of receipt. See Publication 551, Basis of Assets, for more information on the computation of basis when property is received for goods or services.

The term "basis" is familiar to tax geeks, but not so much to normal people. Basis, essentially, is what something is worth in Tax World. If you buy stock for $100, then your basis in the stock is $100. If you buy a car for $1,500, then that car's basis is $1,500. If you add leather seats for $200, then the car's basis is now $1,700. Don't be fooled by these simplistic examples; basis is actually a complex tax topic. The reason basis is important is that it determines your gain or loss when you dispose of property. So, just as with any other property, your basis in the virtual currency is, generally speaking, the fair market value of that currency as of the date you acquired it. More — much more — on this later.

Q-5: How is the fair market value of virtual currency determined?

A-5: For U.S. tax purposes, transactions using virtual currency must be reported in U.S. dollars. Therefore, taxpayers will be required to determine the fair market value of virtual currency in U.S. dollars as of the date of payment or receipt. If a virtual currency is listed on an exchange and the exchange rate is established by market supply and demand, the fair market value of the virtual currency is determined by converting the virtual currency into U.S. dollars (or into another real currency which in turn can be converted into U.S. dollars) at the exchange rate, in a reasonable manner that is consistently applied.

How is that fair market value determined? Easily: just look up the price as of that date on your computer using a blockchain explorer. Not too hard.

Q-6: Does a taxpayer have gain or loss upon an exchange of virtual currency for other property?

A-6: Yes. If the fair market value of property received in exchange for virtual currency exceeds the taxpayer's adjusted basis of the virtual currency, the taxpayer has taxable gain. The taxpayer has a loss if the fair market value of the property received is less than the adjusted basis of the virtual currency. See Publication 544, Sales and Other Dispositions of Assets, for information about the tax treatment of sales and exchanges, such as whether a loss is deductible.

The rubber meets the road here. When you exchange virtual currency for other property, you have effectively sold it. You take the value of that currency on the date you exchanged it (yes, look it up on your computer) and subtract your basis. If the remaining number is positive (it was worth more on the day you exchanged it than on the day you acquired it), you have a gain. If it is negative (it was worth more on the day you acquired it than on the day you exchanged it), you have a loss.

Q-7: What type of gain or loss does a taxpayer realize on the sale or exchange of virtual currency?

A-7: The character of the gain or loss generally depends on whether the virtual currency is a capital asset in the hands of the taxpayer. A taxpayer generally realizes capital gain or loss on the sale or exchange of virtual currency that is a capital asset in the hands of the taxpayer. For example, stocks, bonds, and other investment property are generally capital assets. A taxpayer generally realizes ordinary gain or loss on the sale or exchange of virtual currency that is not a capital asset in the hands of the taxpayer. Inventory and other property held mainly for sale to customers in a trade or business are examples of property that is not a capital asset. See Publication 544 for more information about capital assets and the character of gain or loss.

There are two issues at play here. One is the distinction between long-term and short-term gain or loss. Gain/loss is long-term if you owned it for 366 days or more and short-term if you owned it for less than 366 days.

The other issue is the difference in tax treatment between a capital asset vs inventory vs a personal asset.

For most players in the Cryptoverse, virtual currency is a capital asset because they own it for investment purposes. In that case, you have a capital gain or capital loss, either long-term or short-term, when disposed of.

If you are a money service business and actually do have virtual currency that you are selling to others, then the virtual currency is treated as inventory and your income is going to be ordinary income/losses, not capital gains/losses.

But, in theory, if your virtual currency is used for

personal use (you're spending it), then you'll have to pay tax on any gains, but you won't get to take any losses.

If your eyes just popped open, good. You get the idea. It no different from how any other type of property is treated. If you buy a classic car as an investment and then sell it, you can make a case for this being long-term capital investment gain or loss.

If you're a car dealer and you sell a car, it's ordinary income.

If you're a normal Joe and you sell a car, you have to report income if you have a gain on the car, but you don't get to deduct a loss if you take a loss on the car. That's called the "Heads I Win, Tails You Lose" principle of property taxation.

So far, the IRS hasn't made much of an issue about discriminating between personal gains and losses vs. investment gains and losses, but you can see that they are leaving the door open for that distinction to be made.

Q-8: Does a taxpayer who "mines" virtual currency (for example, uses computer resources to validate Bitcoin transactions and maintain the public Bitcoin transaction ledger) realize gross income upon receipt of the virtual currency resulting from those activities?

A-8: Yes, when a taxpayer successfully "mines" virtual currency, the fair market value of the virtual currency as of the date of receipt is includible in gross income. See Publication 525, Taxable and Nontaxable Income, for more information on taxable income.

Mining is, of course, the process by which virtual currency is born. Or created. Or released. Whatever. It's income. But what type of income? Read on.

Q-9: Is an individual who "mines" virtual currency as a trade or business subject to self-employment tax on the income derived from those activities?

A-9: If a taxpayer's "mining" of virtual currency constitutes a trade or business, and the "mining" activity is not undertaken by the taxpayer as an employee, the net earnings from self-employment (generally, gross income derived from carrying on a trade or business less allowable deductions) resulting from those activities constitute self-employment income and are subject to the self-employment tax. See Chapter 10 of Publication 334, *Tax Guide for Small Business*, for more information on self-employment tax and Publication 535, *Business Expenses*, for more information on determining whether expenses are from a business activity carried on to make a profit.

Not just any old income; it's self-employment income, at least if the mining activity rises to the level of a trade or business. Why is this important? Because self-employment income gets its own special tax called FICA tax (aka Social Security and Medicare aka Self-Employment Tax). FICA tax runs about 15.3% of the net gain. This is in addition to regular Federal and State income tax. Note that this applies ONLY if the activity rises to the level of a trade or business. The hobbyist can report income on Schedule 1, but cannot take expenses against that income.

Q-10: Does virtual currency received by an independent contractor for performing services constitute self-employment income?

A-10: Yes. Generally, self-employment income includes all gross income derived by an individual from any trade or business carried on by the individual as other than an employee. Consequently, the fair market value of virtual currency received for services performed as an independent contractor, measured in U.S. dollars as of the date of receipt, constitutes self-employment income and is subject to the self-employment tax. See FS-2007-18, April 2007, *Business or Hobby? Answer Has Implications for Deductions*, for information on determining whether an activity is a business or a hobby.

Just in case you hadn't figured this part out, if you are an independent contractor and you are being paid in virtual currency, this is taxable income. And, yes, it is also subject to FICA tax (aka Social Security and Medicare aka Self-Employment Tax).

Q-11: Does virtual currency paid by an employer as remuneration for services constitute wages for employment tax purposes?

A-11: Yes. Generally, the medium in which remuneration for services is paid is immaterial to the determination of whether the remuneration constitutes wages for employment tax purposes. Consequently, the fair market value of virtual currency paid as wages is subject to federal income tax withholding, Federal Insurance Contributions Act (FICA) tax, and Federal Unemployment Tax Act (FUTA) tax and must be reported on Form W-2, *Wage and Tax Statement*. See Publication 15 (Circular E), *Employer's Tax Guide*, for information on the withholding, depositing, reporting, and paying of employment taxes.

If your employer pays you wages in virtual currency, this is taxed just like regular wages. Again, no different from how you'd report the receipt of any other type of property. If your employer paid you with a 1967 Chevy, the fair market value of that Chevy as of the date you received it would be part of your pay. And yes, the employer must withhold FICA taxes on that fair market value.

Q-12: Is a payment made using virtual currency subject to information reporting?

A-12: A payment made using virtual currency is subject to information reporting to the same extent as any other payment made in property. For example, a person who in the course of a trade or business makes a payment of fixed and determinable income using virtual currency with a value of $600 or more to a U.S. non-exempt recipient in a taxable year is required to report the payment to the IRS and to the payee. Examples of payments of fixed and determinable income include rent, salaries, wages, premiums, annuities, and compensation.

Q-13: Is a person who in the course of a trade or business makes a payment using virtual currency worth $600 or more to an independent contractor for performing services required to file an information return with the IRS?

A-13: Generally, a person who in the course of a trade or business makes a payment of $600 or more in a taxable year to an independent contractor for the performance of services is required to report that payment to the IRS and to the payee on Form 1099-MISC, *Miscellaneous Income*. Payments of virtual currency required to be reported on Form 1099-MISC should be reported using the fair market value of the virtual currency in U.S. dollars as of the date of payment. The payment recipient may have income even if the recipient does not receive a Form 1099-MISC. See the Instructions to Form 1099-MISC and the General Instructions for Certain Information Returns for more information. For payments to non-U.S. persons, see Publication 515, *Withholding of Tax on Nonresident Aliens and Foreign Entities*.

Note that the 1099-MISC has since been replaced by the 1099-NEC form for non-employee compensation. But the concept remains. If, in the course of your business, you pay someone with virtual currency that is worth $600 or more at the time it was paid, then you are required to send a 1099-NEC to that person and to the IRS. This isn't new: you are required to send a 1099-NEC anytime your business pays a non-corporate entity $600 or more in a calendar year.

Q-14: Are payments made using virtual currency subject to backup withholding?

A-14: Payments made using virtual currency are subject to backup withholding to the same extent as other payments made in property. Therefore, payors making reportable payments using virtual currency must solicit a taxpayer identification number (TIN) from the payee. The payor must backup withhold from the payment if a TIN is not obtained prior to payment or if the payor receives notification from the IRS that backup withholding is required. See Publication 1281, *Backup Withholding for Missing and Incorrect Name/TINs*, for more information.

The point being made over and over here is that there is no escape from any tax or reporting requirement just because payment is made in virtual currency rather than US dollars. You still have to pay tax, you still have to withhold FICA, you still have to send in 1099s, and if the person you paid didn't give you a tax identification number, you still have to do back up withholding.

Q-15: Are there IRS information reporting require-ments for a person who settles payments made in virtual currency on behalf of merchants that accept virtual currency from their customers?

A-15: Yes, if certain requirements are met. In general, a third party that contracts with a substantial number of unrelated merchants to settle payments between the merchants and their customers is a third-party settlement organization (TPSO). A TPSO is required to report payments made to a merchant on a Form 1099-K, *Payment Card and Third Party Network Transactions*, if, for the calendar year, both (1) the number of transactions settled for the merchant exceeds 200, and (2) the gross amount of pay-ments made to the merchant exceeds $20,000. When completing Boxes 1, 3, and 5a-1 on the Form 1099-K, transactions where the TPSO settles payments made with virtual currency are aggre-gated with transactions where the TPSO settles payments made with real currency to determine the total amounts to be reported in those boxes. When determining whether the transactions are reportable, the value of the virtual currency is the fair market value of the virtual currency in U.S. dollars on the date of payment. See The Third Party Information Reporting Center, http://www .irs.gov/TaxProfessionalsThird-Party-Reporting -Information-Center, for more information on reporting transactions on Form 1099-K.

These same rules now apply to exchanges. A US exchange will send you and the IRS a 1099-K if you have 200+ transactions with a trading volume of $20,000 or more. If the IRS thinks you haven't reported what's on that 1099K, you'll get an IRS love letter asking about it. The gross amount that you see in Box 1a of the 1099K better show up in your tax return somewhere. Do note that this is the *gross* amount, not necessarily what your gain or loss is.

Q-16: Will taxpayers be subject to penalties for having treated a virtual currency transaction in a manner that is inconsistent with this notice prior to March 25, 2014?

A-16: Taxpayers may be subject to penalties for failure to comply with tax laws. For example, underpayments attributable to virtual currency transactions may be subject to penalties, such as accuracy-related penalties under §6662. In addition, failure to timely or correctly report virtual currency transactions when required to do so may be subject to information reporting penalties under §6721 and §6722. However, penalty relief may be available to taxpayers and persons required to file an information return who are able to establish that the underpayment or failure to properly file information returns is due to reasonable cause.

And here's the really fun part: just because the IRS didn't tell you sooner what the tax requirements were doesn't mean that you are exempt from those tax requirements. You may need to amend past year tax returns in order to stay compliant with tax law.

SECTION 5. DRAFTING INFORMATION

The principal author of this notice is Keith A. Aqui of the Office of Associate Chief Counsel (Income Tax & Accounting). For further information about income tax issues addressed in this notice, please contact Mr. Aqui at (202) 317-4718; for further information about employment tax issues addressed in this notice, please contact

Mr. Neil D. Shepherd at (202) 317-4774; for further information about information reporting issues addressed in this notice, please contact Ms. Adrienne E. Griffin at (202) 317-6845; and for further information regarding foreign currency issues addressed in this notice, please contact Mr. Raymond J. Stahl at (202) 317-6938.

4
Revenue Ruling 2019-24

AFTER THIS GUIDANCE WAS ISSUED back in 2014, there was dead silence from the IRS for five long years. They were peppered with questions from everyone, including the American Institute of Certified Public Accountants, and they managed to ignore everyone, while still complaining that not enough people were reporting crypto transactions on their tax returns.

Finally, in 2019, the IRS issued Revenue Ruling 2019-24 to answer one and only one of the outstanding issues surrounding the taxation of virtual currency. And that issue was the taxation of forks and airdrops.

Following is the text of the Ruling, indented, with my comments shown in bold type.

ISSUES

(1) Does a taxpayer have gross income under § 61 of the Internal Revenue Code (Code) as a result

of a hard fork of a cryptocurrency the taxpayer owns if the taxpayer does not receive units of a new cryptocurrency?

(2) Does a taxpayer have gross income under § 61 as a result of an airdrop of a new cryptocurrency following a hard fork if the taxpayer receives units of new cryptocurrency?

BACKGROUND

Virtual currency is a digital representation of value that functions as a medium of exchange, a unit of account, and a store of value other than a representation of the United States dollar or a foreign currency. Foreign currency is the coin and paper money of a country other than the United States that is designated as legal tender, circulates, and is customarily used and accepted as a medium of exchange in the country of issuance. See 31 C.F.R. § 1010.100(m).

Cryptocurrency is a type of virtual currency that utilizes cryptography to secure transactions that are digitally recorded on a distributed ledger, such as a blockchain. Units of cryptocurrency are generally referred to as coins or tokens. Distributed ledger technology uses independent digital systems to record, share, and synchronize transactions, the details of which are recorded in multiple places at the same time with no central data store or administration functionality.

A hard fork is unique to distributed ledger technology and occurs when a cryptocurrency on a distributed ledger undergoes a protocol change resulting in a permanent diversion from the legacy or existing distributed ledger. A hard fork may result in the creation of a new cryptocurrency on a new distributed ledger in addition to the legacy cryptocurrency on the legacy distributed ledger. Following a hard fork, transactions involving the new cryptocurrency are recorded on the new distributed ledger and transactions involving the legacy cryptocurrency continue to be recorded on the legacy distributed ledger.

An airdrop is a means of distributing units of a cryptocurrency to the distributed ledger addresses of multiple taxpayers. A hard fork followed by an airdrop results in the distribution of units of the new cryptocurrency to addresses containing the legacy cryptocurrency. However, a hard fork is not always followed by an airdrop.

Cryptocurrency from an airdrop generally is received on the date and at the time it is recorded on the distributed ledger. However, a taxpayer may constructively receive cryptocurrency prior to the airdrop being recorded on the distributed ledger. A taxpayer does not have receipt of cryptocurrency when the airdrop is recorded on the distributed ledger if the taxpayer is not able to exercise dominion and control over the cryptocurrency.

For example, a taxpayer does not have dominion and control if the address to which the cryptocurrency is airdropped is contained in a wallet managed through a cryptocurrency exchange and the cryptocurrency exchange does not support the newly-created cryptocurrency such that the airdropped cryptocurrency is not immediately credited to the taxpayer's account at the cryptocurrency exchange. If the taxpayer later acquires the ability to transfer, sell, exchange, or otherwise dispose of the cryptocurrency, the taxpayer is treated as receiving the cryptocurrency at that time.

The IRS here defines forks and airdrops, and clarifies the fact that currency is only constructively received when the taxpayer is able to access that currency.

FACTS

Situation 1: A holds 50 units of Crypto M, a cryptocurrency. On Date 1, the distributed ledger for Crypto M experiences a hard fork, resulting in the creation of Crypto N. Crypto N is not airdropped or otherwise transferred to an account owned or controlled by A.

Situation 2: B holds 50 units of Crypto R, a cryptocurrency. On Date 2, the distributed ledger for Crypto R experiences a hard fork, resulting in the creation of Crypto S. On that date, 25 units of Crypto S are airdropped to B's distributed ledger address and B has the ability to dispose of Crypto S immediately following the airdrop. B now holds 50 units of Crypto R and 25 units of Crypto S. The airdrop of Crypto S is recorded on the distributed ledger on Date 2 at Time 1 and, at that date and time, the fair market value of B's 25 units of Crypto S is $50. B receives the Crypto S solely because B owns Crypto R at the time of the hard fork. After the airdrop, transactions involving Crypto S are recorded on the new distributed ledger and transactions involving Crypto R continue to be recorded on the legacy distributed ledger.

LAW AND ANALYSIS

Section 61(a)(3) provides that, except as otherwise provided by law, gross income means all income from whatever source derived, including gains from dealings in property. Under § 61, all gains or undeniable accessions to wealth, clearly realized, over which a taxpayer has complete dominion, are included in gross income. See Commissioner v. Glenshaw Glass Co., 348 U.S. 426, 431 (1955). In general, income is ordinary unless it is gain from the sale or exchange of a capital asset or a special rule applies. See, e.g., §§ 1222, 1231, 1234A.

Section 1011 of the Code provides that a taxpayer's adjusted basis for determining the gain or loss from the sale or exchange of property is the cost or other basis determined under § 1012 of the Code, adjusted to the extent provided under § 1016 of the Code. When a taxpayer receives property that is not purchased, unless otherwise provided in the Code, the taxpayer's basis in the property received is determined by reference to the amount included in gross income, which is the fair market value of the property when the property is received. See generally §§ 61 and 1011; see also § 1.61-2(d)(2)(i).

Section 451 of the Code provides that a taxpayer using the cash method of accounting includes an amount in gross income in the taxable year it is actually or constructively received. See §§ 1.451-1 and 1.451-2. A taxpayer using an accrual method of accounting generally includes an amount in gross income no later than the taxable year in which all the events have occurred which fix the right to receive such amount. See § 451.

Situation 1: A did not receive units of the new cryptocurrency, Crypto N, from the hard fork; therefore, A does not have an accession to wealth and does not have gross income under § 61 as a result of the hard fork.

Situation 2: B received a new asset, Crypto S, in the airdrop following the hard fork; therefore, B has an accession to wealth and has ordinary income in the taxable year in which the Crypto S is received. See §§ 61 and 451. B has dominion and control of Crypto S at the time of the airdrop, when it is recorded on the distributed ledger, because B immediately has the ability to dispose of Crypto S. The amount included in gross income is $50, the fair market value of B's 25 units of Crypto S when the airdrop is recorded on the distributed ledger. B's basis in Crypto S is $50, the amount of income recognized. See §§ 61, 1011, and 1.61-2(d)(2)(i).

Here we learn that the amount of income to be reported is the fair market value of that new currency as of the date received. The problem with this, of course, is that the fair market value of this currency may not be easily determined as of that date if it's a new product. You'll have to do the best you can to determine and document the fair market value as soon as possible after receipt.

That fair market value then becomes your basis in that currency, and you'll have a capital gain or loss when you sell this currency. The income from a fork or airdrop is ordinary income, not a capital gain.

Note this means that a third party can create income for you without your knowledge or consent, simply by forking a network or creating an airdrop. Don't get upset by this; the same is true of everyone who holds stocks. Dividends show up without notice, and these are generally subject to tax.

HOLDINGS

(1) A taxpayer does not have gross income under § 61 as a result of a hard fork of a cryptocurrency the taxpayer owns if the taxpayer does not receive units of a new cryptocurrency. (2) A taxpayer has gross income, ordinary in character, under § 61 as a result of an airdrop of a new cryptocurrency following a hard fork if the taxpayer receives units of new cryptocurrency.

DRAFTING INFORMATION

The principal author of this revenue ruling is Suzanne R. Sinno of the Office of Associate Chief Counsel (Income Tax & Accounting). For further information regarding the revenue ruling, contact Ms. Sinno at (202) 317-4718 (not a toll-free number).

This Notice does not have a retroactive statement, so presumably tax returns filed prior to 2019 are not required to abide by it. Presumably, then, those who chose, in earlier years, to take a basis of zero on forked or airdropped currency and report a capital gain or loss only when sold need not amend their returns.

5
IRS Online FAQs

TOWARD THE END OF 2019, the IRS published an online document called Frequently Asked Questions on Virtual Currency Transactions. Here's the url: www .irs.gov/individuals/international-taxpayers/frequently -asked-questions-on-virtual-currency-transactions.

As with all online IRS documents, it's subject to change without notice. One day it says one thing and the next day it says something else.

Equally disconcerting, traditionally online FAQs have not been considered reliable guidance in, say, an audit situation. However, quite recently the IRS did a bit of a turnabout, saying: "Notwithstanding the non-precedential nature of FAQs, a taxpayer's reasonable reliance on an FAQ (even one that is subsequently updated or modified) is relevant and will be considered in determining whether certain penalties apply. Taxpayers who show that they relied in good faith on an FAQ and that their reliance was reasonable based on all the facts and circumstances will not be subject to a penalty that provides a reasonable cause standard for relief, including a negligence penalty or other accuracy-related penalty, to the extent that reliance results in an underpayment of tax."

So that helps.

Here's the complete list of the FAQs as of the time of this publication. Many of the FAQs are a repeat of earlier guidance; I've **bolded** the FAQs that actually added something to our limits IRS guidance, so you don't have to read through all of them.

Frequently Asked Questions on Virtual Currency Transactions

In 2014, the IRS issued Notice 2014-21, 2014-16 I.R.B. 938 (PDF), explaining that virtual currency is treated as property for Federal income tax purposes and providing examples of how longstanding tax principles applicable to transactions involving property apply to virtual currency. The frequently asked questions ("FAQs") below expand upon the examples provided in Notice 2014-21 and apply those same longstanding tax principles to additional situations.

Comments on these FAQs may be submitted electronically via email to Notice.Comments@irscounsel.treas.gov. The email should include "FAQs on Virtual Currency" in the subject line. All comments submitted by the public will be available for public inspection and copying in their entirety.

Note: Except as otherwise noted, these FAQs apply only to taxpayers who hold virtual currency as a capital asset. For more information on the definition of a capital asset, examples of what is and is not a capital asset, and the tax treatment of property transactions generally, see Publication 544, Sales and Other Dispositions of Assets.

Q1. What is virtual currency?

A1. Virtual currency is a digital representation of value, other than a representation of the U.S. dollar or a foreign currency ("real currency"), that functions as a unit of account, a store of value, and a medium of exchange. Some virtual currencies are convertible, which means that they have an equivalent value in real currency or act as a substitute for real currency. The IRS uses the term "virtual currency" in these FAQs to describe the various types of convertible virtual currency that are used as a medium of exchange, such as digital currency and cryptocurrency. Regardless of the label applied, if a particular asset has the characteristics of virtual currency, it will be treated as virtual currency for Federal income tax purposes.

❧

Q2. How is virtual currency treated for Federal income tax purposes?

A2. Virtual currency is treated as property and general tax principles applicable to property transactions apply to transactions using virtual currency. For more information on the tax treatment of virtual currency, see Notice 2014-21. For more information on the tax treatment of property transactions, see Publication 544, Sales and Other Dispositions of Assets.

❧

Q3. What is cryptocurrency?

A3. Cryptocurrency is a type of virtual currency that uses cryptography to secure transactions that are digitally recorded on a distributed ledger, such as a blockchain. A transaction involving cryptocurrency that is recorded on a distributed ledger is referred to as an "on-chain" transaction; a transaction that is not recorded on the distributed ledger is referred to as an "off-chain" transaction.

❧

Q4. Will I recognize a gain or loss when I sell my virtual currency for real currency?

A4. Yes. When you sell virtual currency, you must recognize any capital gain or loss on the sale, subject to any limitations on the deductibility of capital losses. For more information on capital assets, capital gains, and capital losses, see Publication 544, Sales and Other Dispositions of Assets

❧

Q5. The 2020 Form 1040 asks whether at any time during 2020, I received, sold, sent, exchanged, or otherwise acquired any financial interest in any virtual currency. During 2020, I purchased virtual currency with real currency and had no other virtual currency transactions during the year. Must I answer yes to the Form 1040 question? (3/2/2021)

A5. No. If your only transactions involving virtual currency during 2020 were purchases of virtual currency with real currency, you are not required to answer yes to the Form 1040 question.

❧

Q5(a). The 2021 Form 1040 asks whether at any time during 2021, I received, sold, sent, exchanged, or otherwise disposed of any financial interest in any virtual currency. During 2020, I purchased virtual currency with real currency and had no other virtual currency transactions during the year. How do I answer the question on the Form 1040? (updated March 10, 2022)

A5(a): If your only transactions involving virtual currency during 2021 were purchases of virtual currency with real currency, you are not required to answer "yes" to the Form 1040 question and should, instead, check the "no" box.

ↂ

Q6. How do I determine if my gain or loss is a short-term or long-term capital gain or loss?

A6. If you held the virtual currency for one year or less before selling or exchanging the virtual currency, then you will have a short-term capital gain or loss. If you held the virtual currency for more than one year before selling or exchanging it, then you will have a long-term capital gain or loss. The period during which you held the virtual currency (known as the "holding period") begins on the day after you acquired the virtual currency and ends on the day you sell or exchange the virtual currency. For more information on short-term and long-term capital

gains and losses, see Publication 544, Sales and Other
Dispositions of Assets.

❧

Q7. How do I calculate my gain or loss when I sell virtual
currency for real currency?

A7. Your gain or loss will be the difference between your
adjusted basis in the virtual currency and the amount
you received in exchange for the virtual currency, which
you should report on your Federal income tax return in
U.S. dollars. For more information on gain or loss from
sales or exchanges, see Publication 544, Sales and Other
Dispositions of Assets.

❧

Q8. How do I determine my basis in virtual currency I
purchased with real currency?

A8. Your basis (also known as your "cost basis") is the
amount you spent to acquire the virtual currency,
including fees, commissions and other acquisition costs
in U.S. dollars. Your adjusted basis is your basis increased
by certain expenditures and decreased by certain deductions or credits in U.S. dollars. For more information on
basis, see Publication 551, Basis of Assets.

❧

Q9. Do I have income if I provide someone with a service and that person pays me with virtual currency?

A9. Yes. When you receive property, including virtual currency, in exchange for performing services, whether or not you perform the services as an employee, you recognize ordinary income. For more information on compensation for services, see Publication 525, Taxable and Nontaxable Income.

❧

Q10. Does virtual currency received by an independent contractor for performing services constitute self-employment income?

A10. Yes. Generally, self-employment income includes all gross income derived by an individual from any trade or business carried on by the individual as other than an employee. Consequently, the fair market value of virtual currency received for services performed as an independent contractor, measured in U.S. dollars as of the date of receipt, constitutes self-employment income and is subject to the self-employment tax.

❧

Q11. Does virtual currency paid by an employer as remuneration for services constitute wages for employment tax purposes?

A11. Yes. Generally, the medium in which remuneration for services is paid is immaterial to the determination of whether the remuneration constitutes wages for employment tax purposes. Consequently, the fair market value of virtual currency paid as wages, measured in U.S. dollars at the date of receipt, is subject to Federal income tax withholding, Federal Insurance Contributions Act (FICA) tax, and Federal Unemployment Tax Act (FUTA) tax and must be reported on Form W-2, Wage and Tax Statement. See Publication 15 (Circular E), Employer's Tax Guide, for information on the withholding, depositing, reporting, and paying of employment taxes.

რ

Q12. How do I calculate my income if I provide a service and receive payment in virtual currency?

A12. The amount of income you must recognize is the fair market value of the virtual currency, in U.S. dollars, when received. In an on-chain transaction you receive the virtual currency on the date and at the time the transaction is recorded on the distributed ledger.

❦

Q13. How do I determine my basis in virtual currency I receive for services I've provided?

A13. If, as part of an arm's length transaction, you provided someone with services and received virtual currency in exchange, your basis in that virtual currency is the fair market value of the virtual currency, in U.S. dollars, when the virtual currency is received. For more information on basis, see Publication 551, Basis of Assets.

❦

Q14. Will I recognize a gain or loss if I pay someone with virtual currency for providing me with a service?

A14. Yes. If you pay for a service using virtual currency that you hold as a capital asset, then you have exchanged a capital asset for that service and will have a capital gain or loss. For more information on capital gains and capital losses, see Publication 544, Sales and Other Dispositions of Assets.

❦

Q15. How do I calculate my gain or loss when I pay for services using virtual currency?

A15. Your gain or loss is the difference between the fair market value of the services you received and your adjusted basis in the virtual currency exchanged. For more information on gain or loss from sales or exchanges, see Publication 544, Sales and Other Dispositions of Assets.

❧

Q16. Will I recognize a gain or loss if I exchange my virtual currency for other property?

A16. Yes. If you exchange virtual currency held as a capital asset for other property, including for goods or for another virtual currency, you will recognize a capital gain or loss. For more information on capital gains and capital losses, see Publication 544, Sales and Other Dispositions of Assets.

❧

Q17. How do I calculate my gain or loss when I exchange my virtual currency for other property?

A17. Your gain or loss is the difference between the fair market value of the property you received and your adjusted basis in the virtual currency exchanged. For more information on gain or loss from sales or exchanges, see Publication 544, Sales and Other Dispositions of Assets.

❧

Q18. How do I determine my basis in property I've received in exchange for virtual currency?

A18. If, as part of an arm's length transaction, you transferred virtual currency to someone and received other property in exchange, your basis in that property is its fair market value at the time of the exchange. For more information on basis, see Publication 551, Basis of Assets.

❧

Q19. Will I recognize a gain or loss if I sell or exchange property (other than U.S. dollars) for virtual currency?

A19. Yes. If you transfer property held as a capital asset in exchange for virtual currency, you will recognize a capital gain or loss. If you transfer property that is not a capital asset in exchange for virtual currency, you will recognize an ordinary gain or loss. For more information on gains and losses, see Publication 544, Sales and Other Dispositions of Assets.

↷

Q20. How do I calculate my gain or loss when I exchange property for virtual currency?

A20. Your gain or loss is the difference between the fair market value of the virtual currency when received (in general, when the transaction is recorded on the distributed ledger) and your adjusted basis in the property exchanged. For more information on gain or loss from sales or exchanges, see Publication 544, Sales and Other Dispositions of Assets.

↷

Q21. How do I determine my basis in virtual currency that I have received in exchange for property?

A21. If, as part of an arm's length transaction, you transferred property to someone and received virtual currency in exchange, your basis in that virtual currency is the fair market value of the virtual currency, in U.S. dollars, when the virtual currency is received. For more information on basis, see Publication 551, Basis of Assets.

ↄ

Q22. One of my cryptocurrencies went through a hard fork but I did not receive any new cryptocurrency. Do I have income?

A22. A hard fork occurs when a cryptocurrency undergoes a protocol change resulting in a permanent diversion from the legacy distributed ledger. This may result in the creation of a new cryptocurrency on a new distributed ledger in addition to the legacy cryptocurrency on the legacy distributed ledger. If your cryptocurrency went through a hard fork, but you did not receive any new cryptocurrency, whether through an airdrop (a distribution of cryptocurrency to multiple taxpayers' distributed ledger addresses) or some other kind of transfer, you don't have taxable income.

ↄ

Q23. One of my cryptocurrencies went through a hard fork followed by an airdrop and I received new cryptocurrency. Do I have income?

A23. If a hard fork is followed by an airdrop and you receive new cryptocurrency, you will have taxable income in the taxable year you receive that cryptocurrency.

☙

Q24. How do I calculate my income from cryptocurrency I received following a hard fork?

A24. When you receive cryptocurrency from an airdrop following a hard fork, you will have ordinary income equal to the fair market value of the new cryptocurrency when it is received, which is when the transaction is recorded on the distributed ledger, provided you have dominion and control over the cryptocurrency so that you can transfer, sell, exchange, or otherwise dispose of the cryptocurrency.

☙

Q25. How do I determine my basis in cryptocurrency I received following a hard fork?

A25. If you receive cryptocurrency from an airdrop following a hard fork, your basis in that cryptocurrency is equal to the amount you included in income on your Federal income tax return. The amount included in income is the fair market value of the cryptocurrency when you received it. You have received the cryptocurrency when you can transfer, sell, exchange, or otherwise dispose of it, which is generally the date and time the airdrop is recorded on the distributed ledger. See Rev. Rul. 2019-24 (PDF). For more information on basis, see Publication 551, Basis of Assets.

☙

Q26. I received cryptocurrency through a platform for trading cryptocurrency; that is, through a cryptocurrency exchange. How do I determine the cryptocurrency's fair market value at the time of receipt?

A26. If you receive cryptocurrency in a transaction facilitated by a cryptocurrency exchange, the value of the cryptocurrency is the amount that is recorded by the cryptocurrency exchange for that transaction in U.S. dollars. If the transaction is facilitated by a centralized or decentralized cryptocurrency exchange but is not recorded on a distributed ledger or is otherwise an off-chain transaction, then the fair market value is the amount the cryptocurrency was trading for on the exchange at the date and time the transaction would have been recorded on the ledger if it had been an on-chain transaction.

☙

Q27. I received cryptocurrency in a peer-to-peer transaction or some other type of transaction that did not involve a cryptocurrency exchange. How do I determine the cryptocurrency's fair market value at the time of receipt?

A27. If you receive cryptocurrency in a peer-to-peer transaction or some other transaction not facilitated by a cryptocurrency exchange, the fair market value of the cryptocurrency is determined as of the date and time the transaction is recorded on the distributed ledger, or would have been recorded on the ledger if it had been an on-chain transaction. The IRS will accept as evidence of fair market value the value as determined by a cryptocurrency or blockchain explorer that analyzes worldwide indices of a cryptocurrency and calculates the value of the cryptocurrency at an exact date and time. If you do not use an explorer value, you must establish that the value you used is an accurate representation of the cryptocurrency's fair market value.

ᔕᕈ

Q28. I received cryptocurrency that does not have a published value in exchange for property or services. How do I determine the cryptocurrency's fair market value?

A28. When you receive cryptocurrency in exchange for property or services, and that cryptocurrency is not traded on any cryptocurrency exchange and does not have a published value, then the fair market value of the cryptocurrency received is equal to the fair market value of the property or services exchanged for the cryptocurrency when the transaction occurs.

ᔕᕈ

Q29. When does my holding period start for cryptocurrency I receive?

A29. Your holding period begins the day after it is received. For more information on holding periods, see Publication 544, Sales and Other Dispositions of Assets.

ево

Q30. Do I have income when a soft fork of cryptocurrency I own occurs?

A30. No. A soft fork occurs when a distributed ledger undergoes a protocol change that does not result in a diversion of the ledger and thus does not result in the creation of a new cryptocurrency. Because soft forks do not result in you receiving new cryptocurrency, you will be in the same position you were in prior to the soft fork, meaning that the soft fork will not result in any income to you.

ево

Q31. I received virtual currency as a bona fide gift. Do I have income?

A31. No. If you receive virtual currency as a bona fide gift, you will not recognize income until you sell, exchange, or otherwise dispose of that virtual currency. For more information about gifts, see Publication 559, Survivors, Executors, and Administrators.

〇〇

Q32. How do I determine my basis in virtual currency that I received as a bona fide gift?

A32. Your basis in virtual currency received as a bona fide gift differs depending on whether you will have a gain or a loss when you sell or dispose of it. For purposes of determining whether you have a gain, your basis is equal to the donor's basis, plus any gift tax the donor paid on the gift. For purposes of determining whether you have a loss, your basis is equal to the lesser of the donor's basis or the fair market value of the virtual currency at the time you received the gift. If you do not have any documentation to substantiate the donor's basis, then your basis is zero. For more information on basis of property received as a gift, see Publication 551, Basis of Assets.

〇〇

Q33. What is my holding period for virtual currency that I received as a gift?

A33. Your holding period in virtual currency received as a gift includes the time that the virtual currency was held by the person from whom you received the gift. However, if you do not have documentation substantiating that person's holding period, then your holding period begins the day after you receive the gift. For more information on holding periods, see Publication 544, Sales and Other Dispositions of Assets.

❧

Q34. If I donate virtual currency to a charity, will I have to recognize income, gain, or loss?

A34. If you donate virtual currency to a charitable organization described in Internal Revenue Code Section 170(c), you will not recognize income, gain, or loss from the donation. For more information on charitable contributions, see Publication 526, Charitable Contributions.

❧

Q35. How do I calculate my charitable contribution deduction when I donate virtual currency?

A35. Your charitable contribution deduction is generally equal to the fair market value of the virtual currency at the time of the donation if you have held the virtual currency for more than one year. If you have held the virtual currency for one year or less at the time of the donation, your deduction is the lesser of your basis in the virtual currency or the virtual currency's fair market value at the time of the contribution. For more information on charitable contribution deductions, see Publication 526, Charitable Contributions.

જી

Q36. When my charitable organization accepts virtual currency donations, what are my donor acknowledgment responsibilities? (12/2019)

A36. A charitable organization can assist a donor by providing the contemporaneous written acknowledgment that the donor must obtain if claiming a deduction of $250 or more for the virtual currency donation. See Publication 1771, Charitable Contributions Substantiation and Disclosure Requirements (PDF), for more information.

A charitable organization is generally required to sign the donor's Form 8283, Noncash Charitable Contributions, acknowledging receipt of charitable deduction property if the donor is claiming a deduction of more than $5,000 and if the donor presents the Form

8283 to the organization for signature to substantiate the tax deduction. The signature of the donee on Form 8283 does not represent concurrence in the appraised value of the contributed property. The signature represents acknowledgement of receipt of the property described in Form 8283 on the date specified and that the donee understands the information reporting requirements imposed by section 6050L on dispositions of the donated property (see discussion of Form 8282 in FAQ 36). See Form 8283 instructions for more information. (12/2019)

❧

Q37. When my charitable organization accepts virtual currency donations, what are my IRS reporting requirements? (12/2019)

A37. A charitable organization that receives virtual currency should treat the donation as a noncash contribution. See Publication 526, Charitable Contributions, for more information. Tax-exempt charity responsibilities include the following:

- Charities report non-cash contributions on a Form 990-series annual return and its associated Schedule M, if applicable. Refer to the Form 990 and Schedule M instructions for more information.

- Charities must file Form 8282, Donee Information Return, if they sell, exchange or otherwise dispose of charitable deduction property (or any portion thereof) — such as the sale of virtual currency for real currency as described in FAQ #4 — within three years after the date they originally received the property and give the original donor a copy of the form. See the instructions on Form 8282 for more information. (12/2019)

᪣

Q38. Will I have to recognize income, gain, or loss if I own multiple digital wallets, accounts, or addresses capable of holding virtual currency and transfer my virtual currency from one to another?

A38. No. If you transfer virtual currency from a wallet, address, or account belonging to you, to another wallet, address, or account that also belongs to you, then the transfer is a non-taxable event, even if you receive an information return from an exchange or platform as a result of the transfer.

᪣

Q39. I own multiple units of one kind of virtual currency, some of which were acquired at different times and have different basis amounts. If I sell, exchange, or otherwise dispose of some units of that virtual currency, can I choose which units are deemed sold, exchanged, or otherwise disposed of?

A39. Yes. You may choose which units of virtual currency are deemed to be sold, exchanged, or otherwise disposed of if you can specifically identify which unit or units of virtual currency are involved in the transaction and substantiate your basis in those units.

☙

Q40. How do I identify a specific unit of virtual currency?

A40. You may identify a specific unit of virtual currency either by documenting the specific unit's unique digital identifier such as a private key, public key, and address, or by records showing the transaction information for all units of a specific virtual currency, such as Bitcoin, held in a single account, wallet, or address. This information must show (1) the date and time each unit was acquired, (2) your basis and the fair market value of each unit at the time it was acquired, (3) the date and time each unit was sold, exchanged, or otherwise disposed of, and (4) the fair market value of each unit when sold, exchanged, or disposed of, and the amount of money or the value of property received for each unit.

☙

Q41. How do I account for a sale, exchange, or other disposition of units of virtual currency if I do not specifically identify the units?

A41. If you do not identify specific units of virtual currency, the units are deemed to have been sold, exchanged, or otherwise disposed of in chronological order beginning with the earliest unit of the virtual currency you purchased or acquired; that is, on a first in, first out (FIFO) basis.

☙

Q42. If I engage in a transaction involving virtual currency but do not receive a payee statement or information return such as a Form W-2 or Form 1099, when must I report my income, gain, or loss on my Federal income tax return?

A42. You must report income, gain, or loss from all taxable transactions involving virtual currency on your Federal income tax return for the taxable year of the transaction, regardless of the amount or whether you receive a payee statement or information return.

❧

Q43. Where do I report my capital gain or loss from virtual currency?

A43. You must report most sales and other capital transactions and calculate capital gain or loss in accordance with IRS forms and instructions, including on Form 8949, Sales and Other Dispositions of Capital Assets, and then summarize capital gains and deductible capital losses on Form 1040, Schedule D, Capital Gains and Losses.

❧

Q44. Where do I report my ordinary income from virtual currency?

A44. You must report ordinary income from virtual currency on Form 1040, U.S. Individual Tax Return, Form 1040-SS, Form 1040-NR, or Form 1040, Schedule 1, Additional Income and Adjustments to Income (PDF), as applicable.

❧

Q45. Where can I find more information about the tax treatment of virtual currency?

A45. Information on virtual currency is available at Virtual Currencies (IRS.gov/virtual_currency). Many questions about the tax treatment of virtual currency can be answered by referring to Notice 2014-21 (PDF) and Rev. Rul. 2019-24 (PDF).

გ

Q46. What records do I need to maintain regarding my transactions in virtual currency?

A46. The Internal Revenue Code and regulations require taxpayers to maintain records that are sufficient to establish the positions taken on tax returns. You should therefore maintain, for example, records documenting receipts, sales, exchanges, or other dispositions of virtual currency and the fair market value of the virtual currency.

As an example of how these FAQs change, take another look at Question 5.

გ

Q5. The 2020 Form 1040 asks whether at any time during 2020, I received, sold, sent, exchanged, or otherwise acquired any financial interest in any virtual currency. During 2020, I purchased virtual currency with real currency and had no other virtual currency transactions during the year. Must I answer yes to the Form 1040 question? (3/2/2021)

See the date at the end of the question? Yep, this was added to the FAQs in March of 2021, to try to alleviate the confusion that was produced by the Crypto Question on the 1040.

While a good deal of this may look just like the information we already had, some important changes were disclosed in these FAQs. For the first time ever, the IRS told us what inventory methods we were allowed to use: specific identification and FIFO. And that's all. No LIFO, no average cost.

We also learned that ordinary income (forks, airdrops, and so-called "interest") should be reported as other income on Schedule 1.

The IRS corrected an earlier position by saying "date and time" rather than just "date" when it comes to deciding on the fair market value of a received or disposed of currency.

The IRS confirmed our belief that appreciated virtual currency could be donated as appreciated property; see more on this in Part IV, Chapter 4.

The IRS also confirmed that fees can be added to basis; the fees you paid to purchase and sell your crypto are, essentially, subtracted from your gains or added to your losses.

For the first time, the IRS used the term "blockchain explorer" and confirms that such a tool can be used to determine the fair market value of a cryptocurrency.

6

Tax Cuts and Jobs Act

A §1031 EXCHANGE IS A series of transactions that allow for the disposal of one asset and the acquisition of a replacement asset without generating a tax liability until the final asset is sold.

Up until the passing of the 2017 Tax Cuts and Jobs Act, the phrase "like-kind exchange" was bandied about quite freely in virtual currency circles when discussing the tax implications of trading one sort of virtual currency for another. It was assumed by many virtual currency users and investors that the IRS would allow the application of §1031 exchanges to the trading of virtual currency, so — the theory went — you did not need to report any income if you had simply traded one type of currency for another.

The IRS refused to comment.

However, the 2017 Tax Cuts and Jobs Act put a lid on the whole thing by declaring that like-kind exchanges would hereafter be restricted to real estate. This means that there is no option for utilizing like-kind exchange to defer taxation on virtual currency trades for tax years 2018 and later.

Here's how so-called trading is going to work from here on out: when you trade one virtual currency for another, you have effectively sold the original virtual currency at its fair market value (thus creating a taxable transaction) and purchased the second virtual currency with the proceeds. The second currency has a cost basis equivalent to the fair market value of the first currency at the time of the trade.

Example: let's say you buy some BTC for $265.19 and about six months later, you trade the BTC for some quantity of Ethereum. And let's say that on the day you trade it, the BTC is worth $310.10. You have, effectively, sold that BTC and have a reportable gain of $310.10 – $265.19 = $44.91. Your Ethereum now has a cost basis of $310.10.

What about tax returns filed prior to 2018? Good question. The Chief Counsel put out a memorandum on June 18, 2021, stating: "If completed prior to January 1, 2018, an exchange of (i) Bitcoin for Ether, (ii) Bitcoin for Litecoin, or (iii) Ether for Litecoin does not qualify as a like-kind exchange under §1031."

So we've finally learned that like-kind exchange didn't and doesn't apply to cryptocurrencies. The guidance is pretty late in coming; I guess the IRS thinks better late than never.

7

Chief Counsel Memos

CHIEF COUNSEL OF THE IRS occasionally spends time writing memoranda that may or may not be helpful. The few that we've seen on crypto definitely fall into the latter category, but I include them here for the sake of completeness.

On June 29, 2020, Chief Counsel released a memorandum with this subject line: Taxation of Virtual Currency Received in the Crowdsourcing Labor Market.

Here it is in full, indented:

This memorandum responds to your request for advice regarding the tax consequences for an individual who receives convertible virtual currency for performing microtasks through a crowdsourcing or similar platform.

ISSUE

Is convertible virtual currency received by an individual for performing a microtask through a crowdsourcing or similar platform taxable income?

CONCLUSION

Yes, a taxpayer who receives convertible virtual currency in exchange for performing a microtask through a crowdsourcing platform has received consideration in exchange for performing a service, and the convertible virtual currency received is taxable as ordinary income.

FACTS

A variety of digital platforms now enable individuals or entities to "crowdsource" jobs by using the Internet to outsource assignments to an undefined and often large group of other individuals or entities. A crowdsourcing arrangement may involve three parties referred to in this memorandum as vendors, firms, and workers. Vendors develop a platform upon which firms can broadcast their tasks and workers can accept, perform and/or submit the work.

Certain crowdsourcing platforms specifically facilitate the practice of microtasking, which may involve subdividing larger tasks into smaller tasks and distributing the tasks via online crowd-work platforms. In general, microtasks are simple, menial activities that still require some degree of human interaction beyond the current ability of artificial intelligence.

Virtual currency is a digital representation of value that functions as a medium of exchange, a unit of account, and a store of value other than a representation of the U.S. dollar or a foreign currency. Notice 2014-21; Rev. Rul. 2019-24. Virtual currency that has an equivalent value in real currency, or acts as a substitute for real currency, such as Bitcoin, is referred to as "convertible" virtual currency and is considered property for federal income tax purposes. Notice 2014-21. Accordingly, general tax principles applicable to property transactions apply to transactions involving convertible virtual currency.

Certain microtasking platforms allow those who perform microtasks to receive payments in consideration for completing each micro-task in the form of convertible virtual currency. For example, a firm may offer to pay workers in units of Bitcoin or other convertible virtual currency if the worker processes data or reviews images. Other examples include an offer of convertible virtual currency in exchange for downloading a particular app from an app store and leaving a positive review including a comment, downloading games and reaching certain milestones, completing online quizzes and surveys, or registering accounts with various online services. These types of microtasks may provide individuals with "rewards" in the form of convertible virtual currency. The value of convertible virtual currency paid in exchange for a single microtask often is a small amount that may be less than $1.

LAW AND ANALYSIS

Section 61(a)(1) provides that, except as otherwise provided by law, gross income means all income from whatever source derived, including compensation for services. Under § 61, all gains or undeniable accessions to wealth, clearly realized, over which a taxpayer has complete dominion, are included in gross income. See Commissioner v. Glenshaw Glass Co., 348 U.S. 426, 431 (1955). Section 83(a) provides in general that if, in connection with the performance of services, property is transferred to any person other than the person for whom such services are performed, the excess of the fair market value of the property over the amount (if any) paid for the property, shall be included in the gross income of the person who performed such services in the first taxable year in which the rights to the property are substantially vested. In general, income is ordinary unless it is gain from the sale or exchange of a capital asset or a special rule applies. See, e.g., §§ 1222, 1231, and 1234A. Section 1401 imposes a tax on the self-employment income of individuals.

Because the term "service," for purposes of § 61, is not defined in the Code, the term should be construed "in accord with its ordinary or natural meaning." Smith v. United States, 508 U.S. 223, 228 (1993). A taxpayer who performs a task through a crowdsourcing platform, including a microtask, has performed a service for the party that requested the task with the expectation that he or she will receive compensation. If the taxpayer receives convertible virtual currency for performing the task, regardless of the value and the manner in which it is received, then the taxpayer has been compensated with property. See Notice 2014-21. The convertible virtual currency received must be reported on the taxpayer's income tax return as ordinary income and may be subject to self-employment tax. See §§ 61, 83, and 1401.

The short form? If you get on one of those platforms that pays you a Satoshi or so for clicking on a captcha or watching an ad, or what have you, it's ordinary income unless for some weird reason it rises to the level of a trade of business, in which case it's reported on Schedule C, subject to FICA. It's not clear why anyone thought this was required, but OK.

Then, on March 22, 2021, Chief Counsel issued a memorandum with this subject line: Bitcoin (BTC)/ Bitcoin Cash (BCH) Hard Fork. This occurred back in the summer of 2017; four years later, Chief Counsel releases a memo talking about it. What can I say. Anyway, here it is.

> This Chief Counsel Advice responds to your request for advice regarding the tax conse-quences for an individual who received Bitcoin Cash (BCH) as a result of the Bitcoin (BTC) hard fork on August 1, 2017. This advice may not be used or cited as precedent.

ISSUE

Does a taxpayer who received Bitcoin Cash as a result of the August 1, 2017, Bitcoin hard fork have gross income under section 61 of the Internal Revenue Code (Code)?

CONCLUSION

Yes. A taxpayer who received Bitcoin Cash as a result of the August 1, 2017, Bitcoin hard fork has gross income because the taxpayer had an accession to wealth under section 61 of the Code. See Revenue Ruling 2019-24. The date of receipt and fair market value to be included in income will be dependent on when the taxpayer obtained dominion and control over the Bitcoin Cash.

BACKGROUND

On August 1, 2017, at 9:16 a.m., EDT (13:16, UTC), block 478,558 on the Bitcoin block chain was mined.

This was the last common block shared by both the Bitcoin and Bitcoin Cash distributed ledgers.

Immediately following the mining of block 478,558, Bitcoin miners began mining a block that continued to follow Bitcoin's protocols but was incompatible with Bitcoin Cash's protocols. At the same time, Bitcoin Cash miners began mining a block that followed the Bitcoin Cash protocol but was no longer compatible with Bitcoin's protocols. Beginning at this date and time, holders of Bitcoin Cash were, in general, able to engage in Bitcoin Cash transactions that would not be reflected in the Bitcoin distributed ledger and would have no effect on their Bitcoin holdings.

FACTS

Situation 1
A had sole control over the private key to a distributed ledger address that, as of August 1, 2017, at 9:16 a.m., EDT, held 1 unit of Bitcoin. Following the hard fork, A's distributed ledger address continued to hold 1 unit of Bitcoin while also holding 1 unit of Bitcoin Cash. At that time, A had the ability to initiate a transaction to dispose of some or all of A's Bitcoin Cash holdings.

Situation 2
B is a customer of CEX, a cryptocurrency exchange that provides hosted wallet services. As of August 1, 2017, at 9:16 a.m., EDT, B owned 1 unit of Bitcoin, which was held by CEX in a hosted wallet. CEX had sole control over the private key to a distributed ledger address that, as of August 1, 2017, at 9:16 a.m., EDT, held 100 units of Bitcoin. According to CEX's off-chain, internal

ledger, one unit of the 100 units of Bitcoin was owned by B.

After the hard fork, CEX's distributed ledger address continued to hold 100 units of Bitcoin while also holding 100 units of Bitcoin Cash. CEX, however, was uncertain of Bitcoin Cash's security and long-term viability and chose not to support Bitcoin Cash at the time of the hard fork. As a result, B was unable to buy, sell, send, receive, transfer, or exchange any Bitcoin Cash through B's account with CEX, and CEX did not update its internal ledger to reflect that B owned any Bitcoin Cash. On January 1, 2018, at 1:00 p.m., EDT, CEX initiated support for Bitcoin Cash, allowing B to buy, sell, send, receive, transfer, or exchange Bitcoin Cash, including part or all of the 1 unit in B's account.

DISCUSSION

Section 61(a)(3) provides that, except as otherwise provided by law, gross income means all income from whatever source derived, including gains from dealings in property. Under § 61, all gains or undeniable accessions to wealth, clearly realized, over which a taxpayer has complete dominion, are included in gross income. See Commissioner v. Glenshaw Glass Co., 348 U.S. 426, 431 (1955). A taxpayer owning a cryptocurrency that undergoes a hard fork has received gross income under § 61 if the hard fork results in a new cryptocurrency and the taxpayer actually or constructively receives the new cryptocurrency as a result of the hard fork. I.R.C. § 61; Treas. Reg. § 1.451-2; Rev. Rul. 2019-24.

Revenue Ruling 2019-24 applies the general principles of § 61 to conclude that the receipt of a new cryptocurrency following a hard fork results in income. Specifically, the ruling includes in the facts an airdrop following a hard fork as an example of how a taxpayer could receive new cryptocurrency from a hard fork. The specific means by which the new cryptocurrency is distributed or otherwise made available to a taxpayer following a hard fork does not affect the Revenue Ruling's holding.

Bitcoin underwent a hard fork on August 1, 2017, which resulted in the creation of a new cryptocurrency, Bitcoin Cash. The developers of Bitcoin Cash designed the Bitcoin Cash protocol in such a way that holders of Bitcoin received Bitcoin Cash in a 1:1 ratio based on the transaction history recorded in the shared portion of the Bitcoin/Bitcoin Cash distributed ledger, i.e., blocks 1 through 478,558. Thus, at the time the new Bitcoin Cash protocols went into effect, Bitcoin Cash was effectively distributed to all distributed ledger addresses that held Bitcoin as of block 478,558.

Situation 1

A received 1 unit of Bitcoin Cash at the time of the hard fork and had dominion and control over that unit as evidenced by A's ability to sell, exchange, or transfer the Bitcoin Cash. A has ordinary income in the 2017 taxable year equal to the fair market value of the Bitcoin Cash as of August 1, 2017, at 9:16 a.m., EDT. A can determine the Bitcoin Cash's fair market value using any reasonable method, such as adopting the publicly published price value at a cryptocurrency exchange or cryptocurrency data aggregator.

Situation 2

B did not have dominion and control over any Bitcoin Cash at the time of the hard fork, and therefore did not receive any income from the hard fork at that time. On January 1, 2018, at 1:00 p.m., EDT, CEX initiated support of Bitcoin Cash, allowing B — for the first time — to sell, transfer, or exchange B's 1 unit of Bitcoin Cash. B has ordinary income in the 2018 taxable year equal to the fair market value of the Bitcoin Cash as of January 1, 2018, at 1:00 p.m., EDT. B can determine the fair market value by consulting CEX's pricing data. If CEX lacks such information, B can use any other reasonable method.

Short form? The old doctrine of constructive receipt applies to hard forks. Big whoop — we all knew that already.

On June 8, 2021, Chief Counsel issued a memorandum with this subject line: Applicability of Section 1031 to Exchanges of Bitcoin (BTC) for Ether (ETH), Bitcoin for Litecoin (LTC), and Ether for Litecoin.

Yes, you read this right. This is a 2021 memorandum addressing an issue that was put firmly to bed with the Tax Cuts and Jobs Act of 2018. We were all gasping for guidance on like-kind exchange prior to 2018; having it issued in 2021, when no one cares any longer, is absurd.

However, here's what it says:

This responds to your request for non-taxpayer specific advice regarding the applicability of § 1031 of the Internal Revenue Code ("Code") to exchanges of certain cryptocurrencies completed prior to January 1, 2018.

ISSUE

If completed prior to January 1, 2018, does an exchange of (i) Bitcoin for Ether, (ii) Bitcoin for

Litecoin, or (iii) Ether for Litecoin qualify as a like-kind exchange under § 1031 of the Code?

CONCLUSION

No. If completed prior to January 1, 2018, an exchange of (i) Bitcoin for Ether, (ii) Bitcoin for Litecoin, or (iii) Ether for Litecoin does not qualify as a like-kind exchange under § 1031 of the Code.

BACKGROUND

Virtual currency is a digital representation of value that functions as a medium of exchange, a unit of account, or a store of value other than a representation of the U.S. dollar or a foreign currency. Notice 2014-21; Rev. Rul. 2019-24. Virtual currency that has an equivalent value in real currency, or acts as a substitute for real currency as Bitcoin, is referred to as "convertible" virtual currency and is considered property for federal income tax purposes. Notice 2014-21. Accordingly, general tax principles applicable to property transactions apply to transactions involving convertible virtual currency.

Bitcoin, Ether, and Litecoin are all forms of cryptocurrency, a type of virtual currency that utilizes cryptography to secure transactions that are digitally recorded on a distributed ledger, such as a blockchain. Distributed ledger technology uses independent digital systems to record, share, and synchronize transactions, the details of which are recorded in multiple places at the same time with no central data store or administration functionality. Cryptocurrencies may be used as a method of payment; however, many taxpayers transact in cryptocurrency for investment or other purposes.

Cryptocurrency exchanges are digital platforms that allow users to trade one cryptocurrency for another cryptocurrency, as well as for fiat currencies such as the U.S. dollar. The possible combinations supported by the exchange are known as trading pairs. Major cryptocurrencies like Bitcoin and Ether typically may be traded for any other cryptocurrency and vice versa. However, some cryptocurrencies on a cryptocurrency exchange can be traded for only a limited number of other cryptocurrencies and cannot be traded for fiat currency at all. For example, one popular cryptocurrency exchange supported more than 30 different cryptocurrencies, but almost all of them could be acquired with or traded for only Bitcoin, Ether, or fiat currency. In 2017, there were more than 1,000 different cryptocurrencies in existence.

DISCUSSION

Section 1031(a)(1) of the Code provides that no gain or loss shall be recognized on the exchange of property held for productive use in a trade or business or for investment if such property is exchanged solely for property of like-kind which is to be held either for productive use in a trade or business or for investment. The nonrecognition of gain or loss under § 1031 is intended to apply to transactions where the taxpayer's economic situation following the exchange is essentially the same as it had been before the transaction. H. Rept. 704, 73d Cong., 2d Sess. (1934), 1939-1 C.B. (Part 2) 554, 564. The Tax Cuts and Jobs Act, P.L. 115-97, amended § 1031 to limit like-kind exchange treatment after December 31, 2017, to exchanges of real property. Prior to 2018, section 1031 also applied to certain exchanges of personal property.

Treas. Reg. § 1.1031(a)-1(b) defines "like kind" to mean the nature or character of the property and not the grade or quality. One kind or class of property may not be exchanged for property of a different kind or class. For example, an investor who exchanged gold bullion for silver bullion was required to recognize gain in part because silver is primarily used as an industrial commodity while gold is primarily used as an investment. Rev. Rul. 82-166. Similarly, an investor who exchanged one kind of gold coin for another kind of gold coin was required to recognize a gain because one coin's value was derived from its collectability while the other's value was derived from its metal content. Rev. Rul. 79-143.

BTC/LTC and ETH/LTC In 2016 and 2017, Bitcoin, and to a lesser extent Ether, held a special position within the cryptocurrency market because the vast majority of cryptocurrency-to-fiat trading pairs offered by cryptocurrency exchanges had either Bitcoin or Ether as part of the pair. In other words, an individual seeking to invest in a cryptocurrency other than Bitcoin or Ether, such as Litecoin, would generally need to acquire either Bitcoin or Ether first. Similarly, an individual seeking to liquidate his or her holdings in a cryptocurrency other than Bitcoin or Ether, such as Litecoin, generally would need to exchange those holdings for Bitcoin or Ether first. In contrast, Litecoin's trading pair availability at the time was substantially more limited.

Thus, Bitcoin and Ether played a fundamentally different role from other cryptocurrencies within the broader cryptocurrency market during 2016 and 2017. Unlike other cryptocurrencies, Bitcoin and Ether acted as an on and off-ramp for investments and transactions in other cryptocurrencies. Because of this difference, Bitcoin and Ether each differed in both nature and character from Litecoin. Therefore, Bitcoin and Litecoin (BTC/LTC) do not qualify as like-kind property for purposes of section 1031; nor do Ether and Litecoin (ETH/LTC).

BTC/ETH

As discussed above, Bitcoin and Ether shared a special role in the cryptocurrency market that made them fundamentally different from Litecoin during the relevant years. However, while both cryptocurrencies share similar qualities and uses, they are also fundamentally different from each other because of the difference in overall design, intended use, and actual use. The Bitcoin network is designed to act as a payment network for which Bitcoin acts as the unit of payment. The Ethereum blockchain, on the other hand, was intended to act as a payment network and as a platform for operating smart contracts and other applications, with Ether working as the "fuel" for these features. Thus, although Ether and Bitcoin may both be used to make payments, Ether's additional functionality differentiates Ether from Bitcoin in both nature and character. Therefore, Bitcoin and Ether do not qualify as like-kind property under section 1031.

CONCLUSION

If completed prior to January 1, 2018, an exchange of (i) Bitcoin for Ether, (ii) Bitcoin for Litecoin, or (iii) Ether for Litecoin does not qualify as a like-kind exchange under § 1031. This chief counsel advice is limited to the exchanges involving Bitcoin, Ether, or Litecoin discussed above. This chief counsel advice does not address any other cryptocurrencies, or any other analyses not discussed in this advice. Accordingly, no inferences should be made based on this chief counsel advice that are not explicitly set forth in this advice.

This chief counsel advice may not be used or cited as precedent.

All in all, as you can see, these are mostly a waste of time that could be better spent answering some real crypto tax questions.

8

Tax Principles

AFTER YEARS OF WORKING WITH virtual currency clients, I've boiled all the IRS verbiage down to these essential principles:

1. Virtual currency is treated as property by the IRS. For the tax preparer, this is the single most important principle; all else follows from this.

2. Virtual currency is not foreign currency, so no foreign currency exclusion exists. Yes, El Salvador had made Bitcoin fiat currency, but the IRS has not removed that restriction.

3. Virtual currency is self-employment income when received for services, valued at its fair market value as of the date and time of receipt. This means that this income, net of expenses, is subject to both income tax and FICA tax.

4. Virtual currency is self-employment income when mined, valued at its fair market value as of the date and time of receipt. This means that this income, net of expenses, is subject to both income tax and FICA tax.

5. Virtual currency is treated as wages if paid by an employer, valued at its fair market value as of the date and time of receipt. In theory, this income would be part of an employee's W-2.

6. A taxable gain or loss is created upon the exchange of crypto for other property, including other crypto. This means that if you think you've traded your Bitcoin for a computer, what has actually happened in Tax World is that you sold Bitcoin (taxable event) and with that money, you bought a computer.

7. The character of any gain or loss depends on how the property was held. Most taxpayers are holding cryptocurrency as an investment, so gains and losses will be capital. In the unlikely event that someone is operating as a dealer or exchange, though, it would be inventory.

8. Cryptocurrency received for mining, staking and validating is self-employment income if it rises to the level of a trade or business. Income is the value of the crypto received, as of the date and time of receipt. If it is a trade or business for the taxpayer, then this income is reported on Schedule C and expenses may be taken. If it's really just a hobby or side gig, it's Schedule 1 income and no expenses are taken.

9. Virtual currency is subject to all information reporting and withholding required by the IRS as if the payment was made in fiat currency. This includes 1099Ks, 1099-NECs, W-2s, etc.

10. Forks and airdrops are taxed as ordinary income, valued at the fair market value as of the date and time of access. This income is reported on Schedule 1 as other income.

11. Fees may be added to basis. This includes fees you paid to purchase the currency as well as fees you paid to sell it.

12. A charitable contribution of virtual currency may be treated as a contribution of appreciated property.

13. Permitted inventory methods are FIFO or specific identification. Other inventory methods are disallowed.

Most situations involving the taxation of virtual currency can be handled by one of these principles.

Part III

THE IRS' REIGN
OF TERROR

1

The Crypto Question

THE CRYPTO QUESTION WAS ONE of the IRS' first attempts to get their arms around the Cryptoverse. The hope was that in actually ASKING a taxpayer if they had crypto activities, lying on the tax return by answering NO and not reporting the activity would scare at least some taxpayers into compliance.

In 2019, the crypto question was on Schedule 1 and read: *At any time during 2019, did you receive, sell, send, exchange or otherwise acquire any financial interest in any virtual currency?"*

First, not everyone files Schedule 1 and acquiring virtual currency wasn't a taxable event in any case. Tax preparers rolled their eyes.

In 2020, the crypto question was moved to the front page of the 1040 and read: *"At any time during 2020, did you receive, sell, send, exchange or otherwise acquire any financial interest in any virtual currency?"* So it was in a better place, since everyone has to file the 1040 Form, but it was still a stupid question. The IRS picked up on that eventually and explained, through online FAQ #5, that they really didn't mean you had to answer YES to the crypto question if all you had done was to buy crypto or to simply transfer your crypto from one of your accounts/wallets to another of your accounts/wallets.

For 2021, the question looked like this: "At any time during 2021, did you receive, sell, exchange or otherwise dispose of any financial interest in virtual currency?" The IRS finally clued into the fact that acquiring virtual currency wasn't a taxable event, but disposing of it probably was.

For 2022, we have a completely new question: "At any time during 2022, did you: (a) receive crypto as a reward, award, or compensation; or (b) sell, exchange, gift, or otherwise dispose of a digital asset?"

Hilariously, the American Institute of Certified Public Accountants sent the IRS a letter suggesting that the crypto question read as follows: "At any time during 2022, did you have a taxable event involving virtual currency? See instructions."

Apparently, this was just too easy and straightforward, so the IRS rejected the suggestion.

Here's a summary of what activities should result in a YES to the question:

- Received digital assets as payment for property or services provided;

- Received digital assets ass a result of a reward or award;

- Received digital assets as a result of mining, staking, and similar activities;

- Received digital assets as a result of a hard fork;

- Disposed of digital assets in exchange for property or services;

- Disposed of a digital asset in exchange or trade for another digital asset;

- Sold a digital asset;

- Transferred digital assets for free (without receiving any consideration) as a bona fide gift; or

- Otherwise disposed of any other financial interest in a digital asset

The question of what, exactly, constitutes a digital asset has not been addressed by the IRS, but most tax preparers assume it includes cryptocurrencies, virtual currencies, and NFTs.

A NO response is good if all you did was buy and hold; transfer digital assets from one wallet that you owned to another wallet that you owned; or had no digital asset activities at all.

Be aware that owning stock in a company that owns crypto — such as Coinbase or Greyscale Bitcoin Trust — does not mean you own crypto. It simply means you own stock. Similarly, owning stock in General Motors does not necessarily mean that you own a car.

2

John Doe Summons to Coinbase

BACK IN 2016, THE IRS issued what's called a John Doe Summons to Coinbase, the largest crypto exchange in the U.S.

In that year, Coinbase claimed to have served 5.9 million customers and exchanged $6B (yep, with a "B") worth of Bitcoin.

At the same time, the IRS noted that only between 800 and 900 persons electronically filed a Form 8949, *Sales and Other Dispositions of Capital Assets*, that included a property description that was "likely related to bitcoin" in each of the years 2013 through 2015.

The IRS then served a "John Doe" summons on Coinbase, looking for information from records and documents regarding U.S. persons conducting convertible virtual currency transactions at any time from 2013 through 2015.

A John Doe Summons, in case you haven't heard the term before, is a tool available to the IRS to conduct investigations into taxpayers without knowing the names of those taxpayers. Authorization is typically granted if the IRS can show there's a reasonable basis to presume that a group of people may have broken tax laws and there isn't any other way to get the information.

Coinbase refused to comply, and it went to court. The IRS blinked first, filing a "Notice of Narrowed Summons Request for Enforcement" with the court, narrowing its information request to accounts "with at least the equivalent of $20,000 in any one transaction type (buy, sell, send, or receive) in any one year during the 2013–2015 period." Coinbase stated that this request covered 8.9 million transactions and 14,355 account holders.

Coinbase refused to comply with this narrowed-down version, but the court held that the narrowed summons served the legitimate purpose of investigating the "reporting gap between the number of virtual currency users Coinbase claims to have had during the summons period" and "U.S. bitcoin users reporting gains or losses to the IRS during the summoned years."

The court reasoned that the discrepancy "creates an inference that more Coinbase users are trading bitcoin than reporting gains on their tax returns," indicating the IRS has a legitimate interest in investigating these taxpayers.

3
Letters 6173, 6174, and 6174A

WHAT DID THE IRS DO with the information it received from Coinbase? It sent out a series of letters: 6173, 6174 and 6174-A.

Letter 6173 said:

We have information that you have or had one or more accounts containing virtual currency and may not have met your U.S. tax filing requirements for transactions involving virtual currency, which include cryptocurrency and non-crypto virtual currencies.

Virtual currency is considered property for federal income tax purposes.

Generally, U.S. taxpayers must report all sales, exchanges, and other dispositions of virtual currency.

An exchange of a virtual currency (such as Bitcoin, Ether, etc.) includes the use of the virtual currency to pay for goods, services, or other property, including another virtual currency such as exchanging Bitcoin for Ether. This obligation applies regardless of whether the account is held here in the U.S. or abroad.

For one or more of tax years 2013 through 2017, we haven't received either a federal income tax return or an applicable form or schedule reporting your virtual currency transactions.

What made this particular letter a bit terrifying is that the IRS is stating that it already has information about non-compliance and also already knows that you haven't reported it. Taxpayers receiving this form had to act, and act quickly.

Letters 6174 and 6174-A were quite a bit softer.

We have information that you have or had one or more accounts containing virtual currency but may not know the requirements for reporting transactions involving virtual currency, which include cryptocurrency and non-crypto virtual currencies.

After reviewing the information below, if you believe you didn't accurately report your virtual currency transactions on a federal income tax return, you should file amended returns or delinquent returns if you didn't file a return for one or more taxable years. If you do not accurately report your virtual currency transactions, you may be subject to future civil and criminal enforcement activity.

The only difference between Letter 6174 and Letter 6174-A is the ending. Letter 6174 ends with: *You do not need to respond to this letter.* Letter 6174-A ends with: *You do not need to respond to this letter. Note, however, we may send other correspondence about potential enforcement activity in the future. Right.*

And yes, many non-compliant taxpayers were scared into flying straight by these letters.

4
John Doe Summons to Circle and Kraken

THE IRS HAD SUCH A good time with Coinbase that they've recently decided to enact a sequel.

On March 31, 2021 and April 1, 2021, the IRS filed John Doe Summons on Kraken and Circle. Chuck Rettig, IRS Chief, was quoted: "The John Doe summons is a step to enable the IRS to uncover those who are failing to properly report their virtual currency transactions. We will enforce the law where we find systemic noncompliance or fraud."

A Massachusetts federal court approved the Circle John Doe summons stated that it "expects to work collaboratively with the IRS" in complying with the requirements of the Summons.

A judge in California did **not** grant approval of the Summons received by Kraken, stating that the request was "too broad." However, the Summons was eventually approved by a California federal court.

What we can expect to see is another round of letters from the IRS to the taxpayers "outed" by Circle and Kraken.

5
Operation Hidden Treasure

IN MARCH OF 2021, THE IRS announced the formation of Operation Hidden Treasure. This is a group of IRS agents who are trained in cryptocurrency and virtual currency tracking, and have ben tasked with routing out taxpayer who don't report crypto income on their tax returns.

Carolyn Schenck, the National Fraud Counsel & Assistance Division Counsel for the Office of Chief Counsel, described Operation Hidden Treasure as "all about finding, tracing and attributing crypto to U.S. taxpayers." She stated that the IRS is looking for "tax evasion signatures." These so-called signatures include "structuring" which simply means structuring transactions in increments of less than $10,000 to avoid reporting requirements, and the use of nominees or shell corporations.

As part of this effort, the IRS is teaming up with a variety of vendors who are able to identify such signatures, as well as vendors who are able to analyze and de-anonymize crypto transactions.

Schenck's message for would-be tax evaders is a chilling "We see you."

If you're reading this and haven't come clean on your taxes, be aware that the IRS is dead serious about finding you. Remember that your tax preparer does not have attorney-client privilege, so outing yourself to your accountant is exactly the wrong thing to do. Hire a tax attorney who can help you.

6

Infrastructure & Investment Jobs Act

THE INFRASTRUCTURE & INVESTMENT JOBS Act was signed into law on November 15, 2021. This Act is highly significant for cryptocurrency taxpayers.

The Act requires crypto brokers to furnish information about sales and trades to the IRS, just as if they were stockbrokers. Required information includes the name, address, gross proceeds, sale date, acquisition date and basis if known. This will start with transactions that occur on January 1, 2023.

How will it be reported? There's a rumor that there will be a new form, 1099-DA. (That stands for digital asset, in case you weren't sure.) If not, it may just be plain, old ordinary Form 1099-B.

Also required is the transfer of basis and acquisition date if crypto is moved from one broker to another. Moving crypto off an exchange to a non-brokerage account will trigger a report of that transaction as well. This will let the IRS know that you've moved crypto off an exchange and onto — perhaps — a private wallet.

In addition, the requirement to report the receipt of more than $10,000 in cash on Form 8300, if received in a trade or business, has been expanded to include cryptocurrency. So taxpayers who receive cryptocurrency as payment for work will be required to file that form. Form 8300 asks, among other things, the tax ID number and birthdate of the person who gave you the cash/crypto. Pretty soon we'll be issuing W-9s to our employers as well as employees.

Needless to say, this is a huge win for the IRS in terms of forcing taxpayer compliance. That said, there will still be many individuals who keep their crypto in cold wallets, not on exchanges, and not visible for anyone to see. They can continue to use these assets either just to hold onto or to spend in fairly small amounts, not triggering reporting requirements, in peer-to-peer transactions. Taxpayers who use cash to avoid tax requirements will be familiar with the restrictions.

Part IV

APPLYING THE RULES AND REGS

1
Earning Virtual Currency

MOST PEOPLE WHO EARN VIRTUAL currency are treated as self-employed. These taxpayers file a Schedule C with their 1040 returns and bear the responsibility for paying their own Social Security and Medicare taxes as well as income taxes.

You are required by law to report income even if you have not received documentation such as a 1099-MISC, 1099-NEC or a W-2 from the person who hired you, and even if you received it in cash. (I'm not commenting on the likelihood of you getting caught if you don't report it; I'm just stating the law of Tax World.)

If you function as a retail store or online business and you accept virtual currency as payment for the goods and services you provide, then you're responsible for translating that virtual currency into its dollar value and reporting it as income.

If you aren't sure whether or not you are self-employed the bottom line is this: if the person paying you virtual currency doesn't withhold Social Security and Medicare taxes for you (and does not generate a tax form at the end of the year to tell you how much they withheld) then paying these taxes is up to you. Employees get help in paying these taxes: their employer withholds 6.2% of their wages for Social Security plus 1.45% for Medicare and then matches that amount, sending in a total of 12.4% for Social Security and 2.90% for Medicare. If you don't have an employer paying the other half, then you get to pay that 15.3% tax all by yourself. When you add income tax to that 15.3%, you can find yourself owing quite a bit to the IRS when you file your return.

Your self-employment income is the dollar value of that money at the time of "constructive receipt." Constructive receipt is defined as that moment when the funds are available to the taxpayer without substantial limitations. If a check is available to you but you haven't cashed it, you have nonetheless constructively received it. If a fork has occurred but you don't yet have access for your forked currency (ahem, Bitcoin Cash back in 2017), then you haven't yet constructively received it.

The concept of constructive receipt is an important one in the world of virtual currency because the value of virtual currency can vary substantially. A dollar today is a dollar tomorrow, but a bitcoin today isn't likely to have the same dollar value as a bitcoin tomorrow.

Under the doctrine of constructive receipt, you have received income as soon as the virtual currency hits your wallet or becomes available to you in a similar way. Generally, the exchange you are using will give you the dollar value of that income upon receipt. If you don't have an exchange helping you out, then it becomes entirely your responsibility to determine the value of the received virtual currency, document how you calculated that value, and retain that documentation. It isn't the IRS' job to calculate the income you received; it's your job to figure that out and to prove the value of that income if asked to do so.

Remember that you are required to pay tax on any income you receive, whether or not you spend it. Even if you leave that virtual currency in your wallet for the next ten years, it's still considered taxable income upon receipt. When you do spend the virtual currency there's another taxable event — but let's not get too far ahead.

Of course, being self-employed means you can deduct ordinary and necessary business expenses from your income. Generally speaking, if you work from your home, it's possible that you can deduct part of your home expenses as an office-in-home. A miner isn't likely to qualify for an office-in-home, simply because we all know that your computer is sitting there, doing the work for you. You aren't required to watch it for the income to trickle in and, chances are, that room is used for other purposes than just having that computer sit there, quietly solving blockchain problems.

If you have to purchase equipment or software, you may be able to deduct those expenses. Typical expenses for the miner include computers, ASICs (application-specific integrated circuits), and electricity (if the increase in the electric bill can be documented). Note to tax preparers: those ASICs usually don't have a useful life of more than one year so it's arguable that they should be expensed, not depreciated.

Always retain documentation supporting those expenses; Schedule C is the single most audited form in all of Tax World.

Business expenses are similar for *all small businesses,* and your tax preparer should be able to explain what's deductible and what isn't, even if he or she isn't particularly familiar with virtual currency.

If you owe a substantial amount to the IRS and don't meet the requirements for exceptions, you will also have to pay an underpayment penalty plus interest on both the unpaid tax and the penalty. To avoid penalties and interest, you should make quarterly tax payments throughout the year or increase your federal withholding on income from other sources.

Be proactive: talk to your tax preparer about estimating your income and expenses so that you can make adequate estimated tax payments.

2

Spending Virtual Currency

SINCE VIRTUAL CURRENCY IS CONSIDERED property, every time you spend virtual currency, no matter how small the amount, you have created a taxable transaction. EVERY TIME. As of this writing, the IRS has offered no *de minimis* (this is Latin for "too trivial to be considered;" I use the term because the IRS uses it, not because I want to show off) transaction amount to ease this burden.

This is a serious problem for virtual currency true believers who base their entire financial lives on virtual currency. Every time they buy a cup of coffee with that handy bitcoins-to-dollars debit card, they create a taxable transaction. A better strategy, from the viewpoint of Tax World, would be to periodically convert a larger amount of virtual currency into dollars — perhaps once a week or once a month — thereby limiting the number of transactions you must cope with. I understand that this solution goes against the grain for the true believer, but do consider simplifying your life while waiting for the IRS to cut us some slack.

If you are earning virtual currency and don't want to deal with reporting capital gains, the solution is simply to convert your earnings to dollars immediately upon receipt. You'll still have to report the earnings as income, but you won't have to calculate a gain or loss upon the sale every time you convert some virtual currency into dollars.

It's worth stressing that just because the reporting is onerous doesn't mean the IRS won't require it. The US Government (and, by extension, the IRS) has no interest at all in making life easier for the Cryptoverse.

Notice 2014-21 specifically states that payments made using virtual currency are subject to information reporting. If, in the course of your trade or business, you pay an individual (not a corporation) virtual currency worth $600 or more in a calendar year, you are required to issue that individual Form 1099-NEC and send a copy to the IRS. As with everything else in Tax World, the forms are set up to report in dollars; this means that you'll have to determine the dollar value of the virtual currency you paid out as of the date you paid it. And — you guessed it — you must also retain documentation showing how you calculated that amount.

Notice 2014-21 also specifically states that payment of virtual currency is subject to what's called "backup withholding." If you are going to pay someone virtual currency worth $600 or more in a calendar year and that person has refused to give you a tax ID number (social security number, TIN, or EIN), you are required to withhold 24% of that income and send it to the IRS. (You'll have to send it in dollars; the IRS does not yet accept virtual currency as payment for taxes, though several states do.) Failure to send in backup withholding if you are required to do so is penalized.

Again, be proactive. If you plan to pay someone $600 or more in the course of your trade or business, have that person fill out a Form W-9 before you even begin. Pay no attention to the inevitable whining, and don't let them start work — no matter how eager you both are to start — until that form is completely filled out and signed.

If you are an employer who pays employees in virtual currency, you are responsible for meeting the same payroll reporting requirements as any other employer. You just have to remember to convert the payments of virtual currency into dollars. An employer's failure to file and pay payroll taxes is heavily penalized. These penalties can be levied on the business, the business owner, and any other "responsible parties." I strongly advise you to take payroll reporting and withholding requirements quite seriously.

Paying your household employee in virtual currency is no different than paying that person in dollars. A household employee can be a housekeeper, maid, nanny, gardener, etc. If you pay any one of these workers above a certain amount (which changes annually and can be found in Publication 926, *Household Employer's Tax Guide*, then you are generally required to withhold Social Security and Medicare tax. Typically, the painter, plumber and handyman are independent contractors, so you are not responsible for paying their Social Security and Medicare taxes for them.

Failure to file any of the required forms can lead to penalties under IRC §6721, *Failure to file correct information returns* and §6722, *Failure to furnish correct payee statements*.

Finally, note that if you pay someone in virtual currency who isn't a business associate, nor a household employee, you don't have to send a 1099. But, in the eyes of the IRS, you have just sold virtual currency and that is a taxable transaction. Yes, I know, you think you just moved some crypto from your account to someone else's account, but that's not how the IRS views it. In Tax World, you just sold $800 worth of BTC (or whatever) and gave that person the money.

3
Investing in Virtual Currency

BECAUSE VIRTUAL CURRENCY IS CONSIDERED property, gains and losses that arise from investing in virtual currency must be reported as short-term or long-term gains or losses. The good news is that if you hold virtual currency as an investment for 366 days or more, gains are treated as capital gains and taxed at a favorable rate. That favorable rate can save you thousands of tax dollars.

Short-term gains, meaning gains on currencies and tokens that you've owned for less than 366 days, are taxed as ordinary income. Capital losses can be used to offset capital gains; but, as with stocks or other property, the amount of loss that can be used to offset other types of income is limited to $3,000 per year; the rest is rolled forward and used against future gains. This $3,000 limit was put in place in 1978 and has never been raised. If it *had* been adjusted for inflation, that $3,000 would be $12,000 today. Complain to your Congressperson.

Gain or loss is calculated by subtracting your cost

basis from your proceeds. To use a simple example, let's say that in April of 2015 you purchased ten BTC for $236 each, for a total of $2,360. In May of 2019 you decided to sell these ten BTC for $5,000 each, for a total of $50,000. You have a long-term capital gain of $47,640.

Sale price: $50,000
Cost basis: ($2,360)
Gain: $47,640

Now let's add one small wrinkle: transaction fees. You paid fees when you purchased the BTC, so add these fees to the purchase price. If you paid $46 in fees, your cost basis would be $2,360 + $46 = $2406. You paid fees when you sold the BTC. If your fees were $745, your proceeds would be $50,000 - $745 = $49,255. Your gain would be $49,255 - $2,406 = $46,849. Because you held these BTC for more than one year, you would pay tax at the preferred capital gain rate, rather than at the ordinary income rate.

In this example, you knew your cost basis because either a) you kept a record of it, b) you use a wallet that kept a record of it or c) you looked it up online. That's easy enough. Now, let's say you sold those BTC in May of 2019, but have no idea as to when you purchased them or what you paid for them. Without proof of basis, the IRS can choose to assume a worst-case scenario: a basis of zero and a purchase date of less than a year of the sale date. With these worst-case assumptions, you'd pay tax on the entire gain at ordinary income rates. And that would be unfortunate.

Now consider another example: in April of 2015, you bought five BTC for $236 each, for a total of $1,180, and another five BTC in January of 2019 for $3,600 each, for a total of $18,000. In May of 2019, you sold seven BTC for $5,000 each. How would you calculate your gain?

Your two inventory choices are first-in-first-out (FIFO) or specific identification. For now, let's keep it simple and use the FIFO method, which is the default method.

Using the FIFO inventory method, we first sell the BTC that we first purchased back in April of 2015. Let's ignore fees for the moment, just to keep the math easy. If we sell the 5 BTC for $5,000 each, then our proceeds are $25,000. Our cost basis is $1,180. So our capital gain is $25,000 - $1,180 - $23,280. Again, it's considered long-term because you owned those BTC for more than a year before selling them.

Sale price: $25,000
Cost basis: ($1,180)
Gain: $23,820

But we still have two more BTC to sell, the ones we purchased in January of 2019 for $3,600 each, for a total purchase price of $7,200. We're now selling them for $5,000 each, for a total sale price of $10,000.

Sale price: $10,000
Cost basis: ($7,200)
Gain: $2,800

Because you held these BTC for less than 366 days, the gain will be taxed as a short-term capital gain, aka ordinary income.

So we have $23,820 in long-term gain and $2,800 in short-term gain.

Remember that in Tax World your holding period actually starts the day *after* you purchased the asset and ends on the day you sell it. If you purchased BTC on April 1st, 2018 and sold those same BTC on April 1st, 2019, that would be short-term gain. If you sold it on April 2nd of 2019, it would be long-term gain. Pay close attention to your holding period.

Now for a tougher example. I've limited the number of digits in the number of BTC purchased and sold to make this easier to follow. I'm more interested in having you understand the logic behind this process than nit-picking the exact dollar amounts.

Assume you have made the following purchases:

DATE	BTC	PRICE
August 15, 2015	1.0670	$282.96
September 15, 2015	0.0723	$16.62
October 15, 2015	2.3642	$602.42

And then you have the following sales:

DATE	BTC	PRICE
August 15, 2016	0.1034	$37.10
October 15, 2016	1.0000	$399.48
November 15, 2016	1.2777	$909.67

Your thinking should run like this: OK, I sold 0.1034 BTC on August 15, 2016. Which of the BTC did I sell? Meaning: what did I pay for that BTC and when did I purchase it? Using the FIFO method, I sold 0.1034 of the 1.0670 BTC that I purchased back on August 15, 2015. I know I paid $282.96 for 1.0670 BTC, so how much did the 0.1034 BTC cost? If you divide $282.96 by 1.0670, you quickly discover that the per unit BTC price you paid was $265.19 per BTC. Multiplying that by 0.1034 tells you that 0.1034 BTC cost you $27.42. You sold it for $37.10, so you have a gain of $9.68. Since you didn't wait that extra day, this is a short-term gain.

The next step in your thinking should be this: I sold 1.0000 BTC on October 15, 2016. Again, which BTC did I sell? What did I pay for it and when did I purchase it? Using the FIFO method, I have 1.0670 – 0.1034 = 0.9636 BTC left from that August 15, 2015 purchase. I already know that the per unit price for the BTC I purchased on August 15, 2015 was $265.19. Multiplying that by the 0.9636 BTC gives me $255.54. (Note that you get the same result if you take the full purchase price of $282.96 and subtract the $27.42 that you sold in August 2016.) So I sold 0.9636 BTC worth $255.54; the remaining 1.0000 – 0.9636 = 0.0364 BTC that I sold on October 15, 2016 came from the BTC that I purchased on September 15, 2015. How much did that 0.0364 BTC cost me? The unit price of that BTC was $399.48, so the purchase price of the 0.0364 is $399.48 × 0.0364 = $14.54. Total cost basis of the 1.0000 BTC sold is $255.54 + $14.54 = $270.08. Gain is purchase price minus cost basis: $399.48 – $270.08 = $129.40. And, happily, it's all long-term gain.

Next: I sold 1.2777 BTC on November 15, 2016. Which of my BTC did I sell, what did I pay for it and when did I buy it? Well, I've exhausted the batch purchased on August 15, 2015 and I sold 0.0364 of the batch purchased on September 15, 2015, but I've still got 0.0723 – 0.0364 = 0.0359 BTC from that batch. So first I need to sell that. With a unit price of $399.48, the purchase price of 0.0359 was $399.48 × 0.0359 = $14.34. That accounts for 0.0359 of the BTC sold; I still have to account for the remaining 1.2777 − 0.0359 = 1.2416 BTC sold. That all came from the batch I purchased on October 15, 2015. Again, I calculate the unit price of the October batch by dividing $602.42 by 2.3642 = $254.81. I multiply the $254.81 by 1.2416 to get $316.37. Total cost basis of the BTC sold on November 15, 2016 is $14.34 + $316.37 = $330.71. Since the sales proceeds were $909.67, our gain is $909.67 − $330.71 = $578.96. Again, all long-term gain.

You can see that this gets very complex very quickly. You can do the math by hand, or with Excel or one of its cheaper cousins.

But if the entire above discussion made you feel like you want to pass out, OR you are going to have hundreds of transactions, then you need to get help. There are several software companies that will let you import your csv files directly from your exchange and let you print out a transaction summary that you can just hand to your tax advisor. Some of the better-known ones: TokenTax, BearTax, CryptoTrader.tax, ZenLedger, CoinTracker, and Bitcoin.Tax.

Is the IRS going to accept these summaries as fact? No one knows. That's a court case waiting to happen.

Be aware of a few issues: first, coins, tokens and exchanges are being created faster than the tax software firms can keep up. If you don't want to play fun-with-spreadsheets, then stick with exchanges that are supported by the software of your choice. Also, many of my clients have experienced significant problems with the results of the importing process; fees may not be accounted for, donations and gifts aren't accounted for, and so on. Don't hesitate to use your own knowledge to correct the information that is printed out. Your tax advisor is going to utilize whatever information you give her; don't expect her to be cognizant of the ins and outs of your transactions.

We now know that our inventory options are FIFO or specific identification. With that allowance of specific identification, we have choices as to which coins we've sold.

Let's say you have the following BTC purchases:

LOT DATE	BTC	COST BASIS	PRICE NOW	GAIN (LOSS)
Aug 2015	10	$2,652	$346,223	$343,572
Jan 2018	10	$170,000	$346,223	$176,223
Jan 2019	10	$36,000	$346,223	$310,223

Now, suppose that you wanted to sell 10 BTC in January 2021. Using the FIFO method, you'd sell the ten BTC you purchased in August of 2015, for a long-term gain of $343,572.

Using specific identification, you might instead choose to sell the BTC you purchased in January of 2018 for a long-term gain of $176,223.

It might seem like a no-brainer to pick the option that results in the lowest tax, but it might be that you have reasons for paying the higher capital gains this year. Perhaps next year you'll be in a higher tax bracket and thus a higher capital gains tax bracket. Perhaps you plan to sell even more next year, so you want to get as much income moved from next year to this year as possible.

Interested in more advanced investing? The crypto-asset derivatives market is in the trillions of dollars. A derivative is essentially a gamble, via a contract, on the future price of an asset. Typically, income from derivatives is taxed as ordinary income, or as capital gain.

Certain types of derivatives are taxed at a hybrid 60/40 rate: 60% long-term gains and 40% short-term gains. This type of tax treatment is regulated by the Commodity Futures Trading Commission (CFTC) and is generally applied to investments regulated by that organization. Most crypto derivatives will not qualify.

So for most derivative investors, the short-term gain rate will apply for contracts held for a year or less, and the long-term capital gain rate will apply for contracts held for more than a year.

A tax straddle is a set of offsetting positions, such as a futures contract, a forward contract, or an option on actively traded stock or personal property, that hopes to diminish an investor's risk of loss. The loss realized with respect to a straddle position is deductible only to the extent it exceeds the taxpayer's unrealized gain in the offsetting position. Unused losses are carried forward to the next tax year. Form 6781, *Gains and Losses from Section 1256 Contracts and Straddles*, is used to report each position in actively traded personal property, whether or not it is part of a straddle, on which the taxpayer has unrecognized gain at the end of the tax year.

The tax rules governing straddles are extremely complex and well outside the scope of this book. Straddles are not going to be created by any given individual; these investments will be offered by exchanges and — hopefully — that exchange will provide a reporting form for the tax preparer.

Under mark-to-market rules, courtesy of §475(f), eligible taxpayers are treated as having sold their securities on the last day of the tax year at their fair market value, causing gain or loss to be taken into account for the year. Gain or loss recognized under this rule is taxed as ordinary gain or ordinary loss, reported on Form 8949 and Schedule D. The taxpayer's expenses are considered business expenses and are deductible via Schedule C.

If you're thinking "who cares?" let me explain that an ordinary loss is fully deductible to offset income, thus reducing overall income and resultant tax.

On the other hand, a capital loss will happily reduce

a capital loss to zero, but if there's still some capital loss leftover, only THREE THOUSAND DOLLARS of that loss is permitted to offset other income. The rest is carried forward to the following year.

By the way, that $3,000 limitation was put into place in 1977. If it had been indexed for inflation, that amount would now be just under $15,000. Irritating, right?

So you can see why crypto investors would much rather have ordinary losses than capital losses, and thus why the mark-to-market election sounds like a good idea.

Mark-to-market treatment is generally permitted only to day traders in securities. Day trading is a fairly new phenomenon, by the way, as it's only because of the internet, electronic trading, and discount brokerage firms that day trading is even possible.

Does cryptocurrency trading qualify a taxpayer to make the mark-to-market election? It depends.

As of now, only trading in securities qualifies for mark-to-market... and cryptocurrency is property, not a security, according to the IRS. U.S. Securities and Exchange Commission Chair Gary Gensler has called for virtual currencies to be classified as securities, but until the IRS agrees with his position, mark-to-market is probably not an option for crypto traders.

4
Giving or Donating Virtual Currency

LET'S SAY YOUR FAVORITE CHARITY — any approved 501(c) (3) organization approved by the IRS for tax-deductible donations — is short-sighted and only accepts donations in dollars. So you sell some virtual currency in order to make a donation, potentially incurring either a capital gain or a capital loss, and pay whatever tax is due in the case of the gain. You then would be allowed to deduct the full fair market value of that donation, plus fees involved in the sale. The deduction is allowed up to an amount of 60% percentage of your adjusted gross income. If you donate more than 60% of your adjusted gross income, you can roll the unused donation amount forward for up to five years.

But perhaps this wonderful charitable organization has a merchant account that allows them to accept virtual currency. In this case, you could donate actual virtual currency as PROPERTY. This means that if you had held that virtual currency for one year plus one day or longer, you get to deduct the fair market value of that currency as of the date of the donation, without having to cash it in and pay the capital gains tax. If you donate property that has been held for less than one year and one day, you only get to deduct what you paid for it or what it was worth at the time of the donation, whichever is less.

Be aware, also, that there are reporting requirements involved in the donation of property. If you donate property valued at more than $500, you are required to include Form 8283 with your tax return; it makes sense to assume that this same requirement holds true for virtual currency.

However, if you donate property worth more than $5,000, the IRS rule is that you must get an appraisal of the property (which you must send in with your tax return) and a written and signed acknowledgement from the charity stating the value of the property you donated. There's an exception for this get-an-appraisal requirement for donations of publicly traded stock, since the value of stock is available on the stock exchange. A similar exception has not yet been made for cryptocurrency, so expect to have to get an appraisal if you donate more than $5,000 in crypto.

Remember that charitable donations are itemized deductions; making the donations helps you from a tax standpoint only if you itemize deductions. This is true even if you are a small business filing a Schedule C or filing as an S Corporation. Donations do not reduce the taxable income of the business; they flow over to Schedule A as itemized deductions. If the taxpayer doesn't itemize, then there is no tax benefit to the donation. (A discussion of the karmic benefits of the donation is beyond the scope of this book.)

Then there are those donations that are not tax-deductible. When you give virtual currency to a person or organization that is not a 501(c)(3) organization, you have made a gift, not a donation. No worries for you; as long as you don't give any single person/organization more than $15,000, you have no reporting obligations whatsoever.

If your gift to a person or organization that is not a 501(c)(3) exceeds that amount in value, you have to file Form 709, *United States Gift (and Generation-Skipping Transfer) Tax Return*, but no tax is due from either you or the person to whom you gave the crypto. It's just an information return.

5
Inheriting Virtual Currency

SINCE VIRTUAL CURRENCY IS PROPERTY, it seems reasonable to apply property inheritance rules to virtual currency. And this is entirely good news.

When someone dies, their property generally passes to their beneficiaries with a tax basis equal to the fair market value of that property upon the date of the death, or at an alternate valuation date (exactly six months after death) if the estate executor so chooses. A taxpayer who bought virtual currency when it was inexpensive can pass that currency on to his or her heirs and entirely avoid capital gains tax.

But read the fine print: if the heirs are cunning and give their virtual currency to dear old dad less than a year before his death with the idea of getting it back with a fair market value basis, they will be in for a surprise: the IRS wasn't born yesterday. The heirs will get that currency back with an adjusted basis equal to dear old dad's adjusted basis at the time of his death. Further discussion regarding the adjusted basis of gifted assets is beyond the scope of this book: talk to your tax advisor.

If you inherit virtual currency, document its fair market value as of the date of the decedent's death. If you sell it immediately, you must report the sale, but should incur no taxable gain; you may, in fact, sustain a deductible loss because of the selling fees.

6

Receiving Virtual Currency as a Gift

THERE'S NO TAX TO BE paid if you receive a gift. The person giving the gift, on the other hand, may have to file Form 709, *United States Gift (and Generation-Skipping Transfer) Tax Return*. This form should be filed if someone gives a gift that exceeds $16,000 (that's the 2022 number; it goes up every year or so) per person.

That "per person" is per giver and per recipient. If you want to give your daughter $16,000 worth of crypto, no worries. You don't have to file the form. If you are married, both you and your spouse can each give $16,000, total $32,000, without needing to file the form. If your daughter is married, then you and your spouse can give your daughter and her spouse each $16,000, so now we're at $64,000.

There's no tax due with Form 709. It's purely an information return, letting the government know what happened. Why? Because gifts count against the tax-free amount your estate is allowed to pass on to your heirs.

If, on the other hand, you receive crypto as a gift, there are things you should ask the giver so that you're prepared when you sell or trade that crypto. Specifically:

1. What was the giver's basis, i.e., what did the giver originally pay for this crypto?

2. When did the giver acquire it?

3. What is the fair market value (FMV) of the crypto as of the date and time of the gift?

And the reason you need to know all this is that your gain or loss depends on the answers to these questions.

If the FMV of the property at the time of the gift was the same as or more than the donor's adjusted basis, your basis in the property immediately after the gift will be the same as the giver's basis at the time you received the gift. If the donor paid any gift tax, you should increase your basis by all or part of the gift tax paid, depending on the date of the gift. (This gets complicated, so you'd see your tax preparer if gift tax was paid.)

Let's say your mom gives you BTC today that is currently worth $1,000. Her basis in it, let's say, is $500. Your basis in the BTC then becomes $500. The idea here is that no one gets out of paying tax on the gain just because it was gifted away.

If you sell the crypto at a gain and the FMV of the

crypto on the day and time of the gift was less than the giver's basis, then your basis for gain on its sale or other disposition is the same as the donor's adjusted basis. You don't pay extra tax just because it was gifted at a time when the value was less.

In other words, when property is sold at a gain, the recipient of the gift essentially steps into the shoes of the giver.

This is not the case when gifted property is sold at a loss. If the FMV of the crypto at the time of the gift was less than the giver's basis, then your basis for loss on its sale or other disposition is its FMV at the time of the gift. In other words, for purposes of determining losses, you use the **lesser** of the giver's adjusted basis or the FMV at the time of the gift as your basis.

Let's say dad gives you some ETH that is worth $200 as of the date and time of the gift. He purchased it for $500. You immediately sell it for $200. You do not have a tax loss. Why? Because your basis in the ETH was its FMV at the time of the gift, $200.

If you want a bit and the value drops further, down to $100 and you sell it then, you have a tax loss of $100.

What if you had sold that ETH for something in between the $200 and the $500? Then you have neither a gain nor a loss.

7
Forks, Airdrops, Rewards, Interest, Yield Farming

AN AIRDROP IS TYPICALLY A free distribution of virtual currency to community members. To receive the gift, you might need to hold some minimum number of coins in an online wallet.

Then there are forks. A fork represents a change to the blockchain protocol. There are hard forks and soft forks. A hard fork is a change that renders older versions of that protocol invalid; think of it as a software upgrade that isn't compatible with previous versions of the software. All users must upgrade to the new software.

A soft fork is a software upgrade that is compatible with earlier versions. In Tax World, though, we don't care all that much about what happened to the software and more about the financial result of the fork, because a hard fork will often result in free coins being distributed.

If you receive an airdrop, or if you receive some currency because your currency forked, you have ordinary income as of the date and time that this new currency is available to you, calculated at the fair market value of that currency as of the date and time of availability. Again, this is reported on Schedule 1 as "Other Income."

What you do with that forked or airdropped currency after you receive it does not impact your requirement to report it on Schedule 1.

Bob received airdropped tokens worth $10; the next day he sold then for $50. You'd report $10 on Schedule 1, and a $40 gain on Form 8949, with $50 being the proceeds and $10 being the basis.

Charlie received forked currency worth $500 and gave it all to his son. You'd report $500 on Schedule 1.

See how that works?

Note that if currency is promised to you, but you cannot yet access it, you do not yet have income. It's income only as of the date that you can access it in order to sell it, trade it, whatever.

A new wrinkle in the Cryptoverse is loaning virtual currency to an exchange of some sort and receiving "interest" while the virtual currency is held.

I put the word "interest" in quotes because such payments are not actually considered interest in the true sense of the word. Interest is what's paid to you for the loan of your money, not your property. And since virtual currency is property and you are allowing someone to use that property for some period of time, might it be that the payments are actually rent rather than interest?

It's best not to overthink this. It's neither interest nor rent; it's "Other Income" on Schedule 1.

If you are receiving this income in dollars, then that's what you report; if you are receiving it in virtual currency, then your income is the fair market value of those coins on the date of receipt. Those reported amounts then become the basis of those coins when you eventually sell them; the holding period begins on the date of receipt.

The term "liquidity pools" refers to a collection of digital assets that are locked up in a smart contract. The point of this is to provide liquidity to decentralized exchanges to facilitate peer-to-peer transactions, trades, etc. Assets are always committed to the pool in pairs.

In exchange for providing liquidity, the liquidity provider aka your client receives rewards, which are a portion of the fees that users pay to use the pool. The amount of the rewards varies.

There's also an activity known as "yield farming." This is a more labor-intensive form of investing in a liquidity pool and as a result reaps more rewards.

While the differences between staking, yield farming and providing liquidity are important to the participant, tax preparers really don't need to know a lot of technical details.

What we DO need to know is if there are taxable events that result from a taxpayer participating in these activities.

And the answer is YES. The taxpayer who is putting

assets into the liquidity pool or is yield-farming or staking is receiving rewards of some sort, normally related to the amount of liquidity that taxpayer is providing to the exchange, or the amount of risk involved. These rewards are generally going to be Schedule 1, ordinary income.

Note that rewards may be called "interest" or something else — don't get thrown by this. It's still probably Schedule 1 ordinary income.

There's some possibility that these activities, most likely yield farming, could rise to the level of a trade or business, meaning that the taxpayer is in the BUSINESS of yield farming. In that case these rewards would be considered business income, reported on a Schedule C, and subject to self-employment tax. The only good side of that would be the ability to take business expenses as deductions, but for most taxpayers the benefit of those expenses is not going to outweigh the pain of self-employment tax.

Popular yield-farming platforms are Aave, Curve Finance, Uniswap, Pancake Swap, Venus Protocol, Balancer and Yearn.finance.

Be aware that yield farmers pay gas fees, which probably have the highest impact on their profit. Gas fees are Ethereum blockchain transaction fees. There's no getting around them and they can be quite high. Key point: when a taxpayer pays gas, they are essentially trading property (their crypto) for a service (permission to use the blockchain for a transaction). This is taxed as a sale of that crypto.

8

Wash Sales

A **WASH SALE IS A** situation in which a taxpayer sells a security to reap a tax loss and then immediately buys it again at that low price.

For example, you buy Stock ABC when it's $1,000 a share. It drops to $50 a share, but you are ever hopeful and think it's going to regain its value. You sell it on December 30th at $50 a share, report a tax loss of $1,000 − $50 = $950. Then on January 10th, you sneakily buy Stock ABC back at $50 a share. Nice try, but again, the IRS wasn't born yesterday. Anytime a security is purchased within 30 days of a "substantially identical" security being sold at a loss, that loss is disallowed.

I'm often asked if the wash sale rules apply to virtual currency. The IRS Code in question (§1091) specifically refers to shares of stock or securities, so it's hard to see how the rules applying to wash sales would affect virtual currency without the IRS providing some substantive guidance to that effect. At this point, it seems reasonable to suppose that virtual currency investors are exempt from wash sale rules.

Weirdly, Congress has talked for a while about "closing the wash sale loophole" for crypto. To be clear, it isn't a loophole. It's a result of the IRS classifying crypto as property, rather than as a security. This was actually part of the original Build Back Better Act, but ended up on the cutting room floor.

It's my opinion that this issue won't be reopened again any time soon and it is safe for crypto investors to sell out, harvest tax losses, and then repurchase their positions.

9
Thefts, Hacks, Scams and Rug Pulls

How you'll handle this situation depends on exactly what happened.

If the dog ate the paper your keys were written down on, the IRS isn't going to be too helpful. Same answer if you can't find where you stored the keys on your hard drive. Sometimes stupid is just stupid, and bad luck is just bad luck.

However, if your virtual currency vanished in a defunct exchange or you were the victim of a rug pull, there may be some options.

First, remember that we can no longer take an itemized deduction on Schedule A for theft losses; that went away with the Tax Cuts and Jobs Act.

Form 8949 is specifically **not** allowed for theft of capital assets, so that's out.

I have heard a tax attorney talk about the possibility of using Form 4797, *Sales of Business Property*, and referring to the lost currency as an abandoned asset. This is by no means a tried-and-true method of reporting such losses; hire a tax attorney to help you with this.

Another possibility, if your client was scammed, is to take a Ponzi-type loss on Form 4684, *Casualties and Thefts*. You'd take this loss on Section C of the form: Theft Loss Deduction for Ponzi-Type Investment Scheme Using the Procedures in Revenue Ruling 2009-20.

Expect the IRS to come calling if you go either the Form 4797 or Form 4684 route. Documentation is absolutely crucial. You can't just claim you were scammed and expect to deduct thousands of dollars on the strength of that claim.

Note that losses on virtual currency are the sort of thing the IRS will enjoy auditing; make sure your documentation ducks are all in a row. What did you spend on Worthless Token? Did you remember to report a gain or loss when you "traded" BTC or Ether in order to obtain Worthless? We know you don't have a broker's report, but do you at least have printouts detailing your transactions? Screen shots? These are the sort of things the IRS will want to see.

I would absolutely recommend talking to an attorney before proceeding with either of these options.

Let's talk briefly about rug pulls before leaving this topic. There are typically three different kinds of rug pulls: liquidity stealing, limiting sell orders, and dumping.

Liquidity stealing is when creators of a token withdraw all the coins from the liquidity pool. This drives the price of the token down to zero, and the crypto is now worthless. If this occurs, your best bet is to try to sell them, even for just pennies, so that you can take the loss on Form 8949. If you're not able to sell them even for pennies, you might try the abandoned asset or fraud approach.

Limiting sell orders happens when developers deliberately code the token so that they're the only people who can sell them. If this happens and you literally can't sell the tokens, then Form 8949 is out. Again, try the abandoned asset or fraud approach.

Dumping occurs when the developers very quickly sell off their own supply of tokens, driving the price down and leaving investors with tokens pretty close to worthless. Again, even if you can only get pennies, sell and take the loss. If not, again — try the abandoned asset or fraud approach.

Remember that selling and reporting the loss on Form 8949 will only let you take a $3,000 per year loss against other income, but is unlikely to be scrutinized by the IRS unless the loss is large. Using the abandoned asset or fraud approach allows you to take the loss in full, but will almost certainly bring on IRS scrutiny.

10

Foreign Reporting Requirements

TAXPAYERS WHO HAVE A FINANCIAL interest in or signature authority over foreign financial accounts are required to file Report of Foreign Bank and Financial Accounts (FBAR) with the Financial Crimes Enforcement Network (FinCEN) if the aggregate value of those accounts exceeds $10,000 at any time during the calendar year. So does that mean that holding virtual currency in a foreign exchange requires the filing of an FBAR if the value of that account exceed $10,000 at any point during the year?

In June of 2014, Rod Lundquist, a senior program analyst for the Small Business/Self-Employed Division, stated that "FinCEN has said that virtual currency is not going to be reportable on the FBAR, at least for this filing season."

In July of 2019, the IRS officially confirmed this statement by responding to a direct question from the AICPA Virtual Currency Task Force, stating that

FBARs are not required for virtual currency accounts. Hallelujah.

But wait! We're not done. Here's what FinCEN published on December 30, 2020:

> Currently, the Report of Foreign Bank and Financial Accounts (FBAR) regulations do not define a foreign account holding virtual currency as a type of reportable account. (See 31 CFR 1010.350(c)). For that reason, at this time, a foreign account holding virtual currency is not reportable on the FBAR (unless it is a reportable account under 31 C.F.R. 1010.350 because it holds reportable assets besides virtual currency). However, FinCEN intends to propose to amend the regulations implementing the Bank Secrecy Act (BSA) regarding reports of foreign financial accounts (FBAR) to include virtual currency as a type of reportable account under 31 CFR 1010.350.

We don't know what the timing of this is going to be. We don't know if it's going to be retroactive. We only know that it's coming. At some point, crypto investors with $10K or more in a foreign account will be required to file an FBAR.

The other foreign reporting form is Form 8938. Form 8938 must be filed to report a taxpayer's foreign financial assets if the total value of all these assets is more than the reporting threshold.

That reporting threshold is as follows: if you are unmarried, you must file the form is the total value of the assets on the last day of the year is more than $50,000 or the total value of the assets is more than $75,000 at any time during the year. Those numbers double for married taxpayers filing jointly.

The million-dollar question, of course, is whether or not digital assets held on foreign exchanges are considered foreign assets for Form 8938 purposes.

Instructions for the form talk about financial accounts maintained by a foreign financial institution; stocks issued by someone not a U.S. person; interests in a foreign entity; financial instruments or contracts that have an issuer or counterparty that that is not a U.S. person; notes, bonds, debentures, or other forms of indebtedness issued by a foreign person, an interest in a foreign trust or foreign estate, and more.

Digital assets are not mentioned in the rather long and comprehensive lists in the instructions. At this point, we simply don't know if Form 8938 is meant to be filed to report digital assets or not. There are opinions on the web on both sides of the fence. Certainly, the conservative approach would be to report such assets on this form.

11

Initial Coin/Exchange/ Token Offerings

INITIAL COIN OFFERINGS (ICOs), INITIAL exchange offerings (IEOs), and initial token offerings (ITOs) are the virtual version of IPOs, or initial public offerings. ICOs/ IEOs/ITOs are faster and cheaper than an IPO and can be incredibly profitable for issuers. They are also completely unregulated and can be total scams.

Via an ICO/IEO/ITO, a new digital currency or product is created and sold online, sometimes raising tens of millions of dollars in just minutes. The idea is that this new currency/product/whatever will become the latest virtual currency of choice or will be redeemable for services such as data storage. Just as with IPOs, the investor wants to buy in cheap at the starting gate with the hope that the investment will appreciate over time.

The Securities and Exchange Commission (SEC) has gotten pretty interested in these offerings. In August of 2018 the SEC published a paper stating that ICOs may qualify as an offering of a security, subject to the federal regulations that apply to securities.

"As a general matter, though, ICOs are more likely to qualify as offerings of 'securities' when token purchasers (1) are motivated primarily by a desire for financial returns (as opposed to a desire to use or consume some good or service for which tokens can be exchanged), and (2) lack a meaningful ability to control the activities on which their profits will depend."

The SEC has slapped a number of virtual ICO hands, resulting in hundreds of startups being penalized for violating securities law and then quietly — or not quietly — agreed to refund investors' money and pay fines.

You can see how interesting this is: virtual currencies are considered property per the IRS, but potential securities to the SEC. Again, we're in new territory here, where old definitions don't work.

Payment to get into an ICO/ITO/IEO is usually made with an established virtual currency such as BTC or Ethereum. Your basis in the new coins is equal to your basis in the virtual currency with which you purchased those new coins. Iif you spent $10,000 worth of Bitcoin to buy AmyCoin, then your basis in the AmyCoin is $10,000. And don't forget that you now have a taxable event; you have essentially sold that $10,000 Bitcoin and you may therefore have a gain or a loss, depending on your basis in that Bitcoin.

As ever, record-keeping is essential.

12

Loaning Virtual Currency to a Friend

WHAT ABOUT LOSSES OF VIRTUAL currency that you weren't holding as an investment, but perhaps loaned to a friend? Let's say you loaned 3 BTC to your buddy. It was just a friendly loan, no paperwork, no interest rate, and Buddy vanished, taking the private keys to your BTC with him. Guess what? No help from Tax World. You've got no paper trail, nothing to substantiate your claim that this was a loan and not a gift.

Having wised up, when you loan Sally 2 BTC the following year, you have her sign paperwork stating the terms of repayment, including an interest rate. Alas, Sally suddenly stops answering her phone. You send certified letters (keeping copies), you take her to small claims court (she doesn't show up). Under these circumstances, you've probably got a good claim to a non-business bad debt, which you can take as a short-term capital loss. (Yes, even if these legal shenanigans went on for more than a year, non-business bad debts are always short-term.)

If Sally manages to repay 1 BTC, you can still take a loss for the remaining BTC. If you've already taken the deduction when she pays you, then you have to report the fair market value of the collected BTC as ordinary income.

13
Virtual Currency IRAs and HSAs

THERE IS NO SPECIFIC INDIVIDUAL Retirement Account (IRA) recognized by the Internal Revenue Service (IRS) designed for cryptocurrencies. When you hear about a "cryptocurrency IRA" or "Bitcoin IRA," it simply refers to an IRA that includes digital currencies within its portfolio of holdings

These IRAs are subject to the same income restrictions and requirements. You don't even have to tell your tax preparer that you've investing in virtual currency; just make sure you understand whether that IRA contribution will help your tax situation (deductible) or not (nondeductible). Your tax advisor can help you.

Many HSAs (Health Savings Accounts) will also let you invest your money in cryptocurrencies.

The big advantage to investing in cryptocurrencies via IRAs and HSAs is that you don't have to track the gains and losses for your tax return! It's all going to be taxed as ordinary income when you take it out, so there's no need to report what happens while the money is sheltered under those umbrellas.

The disadvantage is that you may pay higher fees when investing via an HSA or IRA.

A word of caution: there are a lot of scams out there. Both the U.S. Commodities Futures Commission and the Securities and Exchange Commission have issued alerts about fraudulent cryptocurrency IRAs. There have even been crypto companies claiming to be "approved the by IRS." The IRS has no interest in approving investments; if you see that sort of language from an IRA company or custodian, run, do not walk, to the nearest exit.

14

1099-Ks

US EXCHANGES WILL TYPICALLY SEND 1099-K forms to traders who have made 200 or more transactions, the volume of which equals $20,000 or more. The same form is sent to the IRS. Starting in 2022, though, that $20,000 is being dropped to SIX HUNDRED DOLLARS. So you may receive a 1099-K even though you've never seen one before in your life.

There are two interesting issues in connection with receiving a 1099-K from an exchange. First, you'll note that it shows money received, but not money spent. For example, you may have received $250,000 through the exchange, but you may have spent $300,000 buying that virtual currency in the first place. The $250,000 will show up on the 1099-K; the $300,000 will not. The IRS is going to assume that you have $250,000 of income and it's up to you to prove that you don't.

The second interesting issue is this: where do you report that 1099-K number on your tax return? Remember that the IRS' matching program is going to be looking for that gross amount somewhere on the tax return; if it doesn't see it, you'll get a letter from the IRS telling you what the tax is on that $250,000 and requesting payment. So that gross number needs to show up somewhere.

Typically, a 1099-K is issued in conjunction with business income; the matching program may be specifically looking for that number on a Schedule C. If you instead put that gross number on a Form 8949 and thus a Schedule D, then subtract out the basis of those sales, will the matching program be satisfied? We don't know. We hope so.

15
NFTs

NFT STANDS FOR NON-FUNGIBLE TOKEN. The word "non-fungible" means unique and not replaceable with something else. The concept of NFTs is based on what is called a "colored coin." Colored coins are satoshis (small fractions of a Bitcoin) "colored in" with information that can link the coins to real-world assets. These are not coins in any traditional sense of the word; instead, they are small amounts of metadata that represent asset manipulation instructions. If your eyes just glazed over, don't worry; you don't have to understand any of the technical details to apply tax laws to NFTs.

The idea behind an NFT is that ownership of a non-physical thing, such as a piece of digital art, CryptoPunks (characters generated by artificial intelligence), Metaverse (virtual land), etc., can change hands via the transfer of a unique identifier (similar to a serial number), built on a blockchain such as Ethereum. Without this unique identifier, ownership of an intangible asset such as digital art is difficult to prove. With these unique identifiers, however, artists can create and monetize their work with full transparency as to who created and subsequently purchased the artwork. That unique identifier is the NFT.

Thanks to the unbreakable and unfakeable nature of the blockchain, any time the NFT is moved from one owner to another, the blockchain records the date of the transfer and the price paid, and that information is available for anyone and everyone to see. NFTs guarantee the provenance of intangible assets with a level of certainty that is rarely achievable with physical assets.

NFTs also have the potential to eliminate the middleman, linking creators of various types directly to their customers. This puts more money into the hands of the actual artists, rather than having money side-tracked into auction houses, galleries, streaming services and the like. This is, not surprisingly, exactly the sort of thing cryptocurrency hopes to do: link sellers and buyers directly and eliminate the middleman.

And yet another advantage to the NFT is that it is indestructible. When owning a physical asset, there is always risk: your artwork or collectible trading cards could be lost in a fire or a flood. But their digital equivalents, owned via a line of code, are eternal…as long as you don't lose the code!

There are big bucks involved here. In 2021, collectors and traders spent $22 billion — yes, that's billion with a

B — on NFTs, up from $100 million in 2020, according to DappRadar, an NFT trading platform.

At this point in time, it's not clear that the client involved in NFTs will receive any sort of 1099 or similar document. That doesn't mean it isn't taxable income. Understanding the underlying issues thus becomes crucial for the tax preparer.

Art is a natural for NFTs. The first NFT was created by a digital artist named Kevin McCoy on May 3, 2014. The artwork, entitled "Quantum," was created by code; it appears online as a pulsing digital light (you can Google it). It sold for $1.4 million on Sotheby's in June 2021. The most expensive NFT sold to date is "The Merge," which sold for $91.8 million. The purchase price was met by almost 30,000 collectors banding together to become its new owners.

Music can be and is sold via NFTs, and this can be a big plus for musicians. Typically, musicians receive only a fraction of the money that their music generates since a big percentage of that income goes to various middlemen. But selling music via NFTs allows musicians to keep almost all the income. A group called Kings of Leon released an entire album called "When You See Yourself" as an NFT. Tickets to Kings of Leon concerts are also sold via NFTs.

Video clips are being sold via NFTs. A video clip featuring Donald Trump sold in February 2021 for $6.6 million. A 2010 YouTube video called "Charlie

Bit Me" was purchased by a music studio in Dubai for $760,999 in May 2021. (You can still watch "Charlie Bit Me" on YouTube; it's actually pretty funny.) Clips of certain sports moments, such as slamdunks and touchdowns are sold via NFT; a video clip of LeBron dunking a basketball sold for over $208,000.

Video games: in-game assets such as avatars can be purchased and sold via NFTs. Millions of copies of DLC (downloadable content) are sold to players, but an asset sold via NFT is unique and exclusive. Some games allow such assets to be bought and sold in-game; others require NFT creators and purchasers to connect outside the game.

Collectible items are also a natural for NFTs. There are digital trading cards, just like the old-fashioned collectible baseball cards or the more recent Pokemon cards, but digital trading cards have no physical existence. David Beckham's 2012–2013 digital Rare Player Card sold for almost half a million dollars.

Photographs can be bought and sold via NFT. A picture of LeBron James taken by Kimani Okearah on Feb. 1, 2020, is currently on sale on the OpenSea platform for 10,000 Ethereum (ETH), roughly $24 million.

You can buy and sell memes on the NFT market. The most expensive meme to date is the Doge meme, which sold for $4 million. The seller was the owner of Kabuso, the dog from the Doge image. The new owner of the meme then began selling fractional shares of that ownership via tokens that are being called "DOG tokens." This process of selling fractional shares is called "fractionalizing."

If you've ever tried to buy a domain name only to discover that it's been taken, you may have then seen a pop-up offering to negotiate your purchase of that domain name from its owner for a hefty fee. Instead, the domain name can be sold via an NFT, once again eliminating a pricey middleman.

If your online avatar needs a closet upgrade, you can buy virtual fashion via NFT. Burberry and Louis Vuitton are among those providing such NFTs.

Jack Dorsey, the founder of Twitter, sold his first-ever tweet — "just setting up my twttr" — for about $2.9 million in March 2021. The purchaser then tweeted "This is not just a tweet! I think years later people will realize the true value of this tweet, like the Mona Lisa painting." This has not proven true so far — the purchaser has not been able to sell this "Mona Lisa Tweet" for anything even close to what he paid for it.

Now let's get into the tax issues surrounding NFTs. The creation of an asset and its associated NFT does not give rise to a taxable event, just as writing a book and typing "The End" does not create a taxable event. A digital artist may create any number of pieces of digital art without creating a taxable event. A digital musician may record songs without creating a taxable event. A photographer may take many photographs without creating a taxable event. It's only when such assets are sold that we tax preparers get interested.

When the digital asset is sold by the creator, that creator has either Schedule C income or hobby income, depending on whether the activity is engaged in for profit, as dictated by §183. The character of the income is unlikely to change simply because the asset in question has no physical existence and ownership was transferred via an NFT. At this time, it doesn't seem likely that NFT platforms will be subject to information reporting, so no 1099 should be expected.

There may be other types of income for creators. As with cryptocurrency, participators in the NFTverse may receive airdrops of free NFTs. The fair market values of such airdrops are considered ordinary income and are reported on the taxpayer's 1040 on Schedule 1, Line 8z, on the 2021 tax forms. However, the FMV of an airdropped NFT, generally based on a third-party transaction between a willing buyer and a willing seller, may be difficult to determine at this point in time. If the NFT was received for free, the FMV probably isn't much.

NFT creators may also win prizes from contests such as the NFT Awards. As always, the monetary value of a prize (if any) is taxed as ordinary income [§74(a)].

That's the NFT creator — what about an NFT buyer? The initial buyer of an NFT (let's call her Alice) now has an asset with a basis equivalent to the purchase price plus any additional costs incurred in that purchase. If she then sells it to another buyer (let's call him Bob) then Alice has a gain or loss, depending on the sale price, associated fees and her basis. The nature of that gain or loss (capital vs. ordinary vs. collectible) would depend on the underlying asset and the length of time it was held.

Be aware that Alice very likely made this purchase with a cryptocurrency such as Ether (ETH). This purchase is a taxable event for Alice because trading one piece of property (the cryptocurrency) for another piece of property (the NFT) results in a gain or loss.

Perhaps another taxpayer, Bob, purchased the NFT from Alice for business purposes. Maybe he wants to use that piece of digital art in his advertising or wants to use the piece of music as his company's theme song. Since the asset is intangible and being used in a trade or business, we may think that it is subject to amortization. Whether this is actually the case is probably going to depend on exactly what Bob purchased. The issue we have to deal with is the underlying asset, not the intangible NFT itself.

Artwork, for example, neither depreciates nor amortizes, simply because it does not have a determinable useful life. Revenue Ruling 68-232 states: "A valuable and treasured art piece does not have a determinable useful life. While the actual physical condition of the property may influence the value placed on the object, it will not ordinarily limit or determine the useful life. Accordingly, depreciation of works of art generally is not allowable."

If the underlying asset qualifies as a §197 intangible

asset, it may be amortized over 15 years. Intangible assets amortizable under §197 include: goodwill, going concern value, workforce in place, business books and records, patents, copyrights, formulas, processes, designs, patterns, knowhow, formats, customer-based intangibles, supplier-based intangibles, any similar items, licenses, permits, other rights, covenants not to compete, franchises, trademarks or trade names [§197(d)(1)]. If a taxpayer chooses to amortize an NFT, it would be prudent to disclose this choice on the tax return.

But perhaps Bob purchased the NFT for personal reasons. What if he purchased an NFT representing a collectible such as digital trading cards? In that case, his taxable event upon purchase is the trade of his virtual currency for the asset. If he bought the NFT with dollars, there is no taxable event upon purchase.

When he eventually sells the asset, that sale should probably be taxed as a sale of a collectible. Again, we have no IRS regulations to help us out, but we can let the tax treatment of the underlying asset be our guide. Disclosing the position on the tax return would probably be a good idea.

"Gas" fees, which are the fees charged by the NFT platform, are essentially transaction fees. It seems reasonable to add the fees to basis. Note that gas is normally paid in cryptocurrency so — once again — there's a sale of cryptocurrency for sellers and purchasers.

Note that the purchaser of an NFT may have a

requirement to issue the creator a 1099 if that purchase was made directly from the creator and not via a platform.

Tax issues for traders Just as we now have crypto-currency traders, we also have NFT traders. Just as with cryptocurrency, the trade of NFT X for NFT Y should be treated as a sale of NFT X and a purchase of NFT Y, with the gain or loss of the sale depending on the basis, fair market value and associated fees. Again, remember there will be gas on these trades, paid via cryptocurrency. Again, at this point, we don't know what reporting requirements, if any, from the Infrastructure and Investment Jobs Act will apply to NFT platforms.

Licensers also have tax issues. Understand that the use of the NFT's underlying asset can be licensed, which generates ordinary income for its owner. NFT license agreements function just as any other license agreement, protecting the property rights and financial interests of NFT owners.

NFT license agreements are coded into the NFT blockchain and function as smart contracts. The smart contract is designed to certify the authenticity of the NFT (so that the licensee knows the ownership is real) and to automatically execute NFT license terms.

Such a license can funnel income to the creator, the purchaser or both. The terms of the original contract between the creator and the purchaser may include the creator's right to a certain amount of income via licensing.

How are royalties from such licensing efforts taxed? Again, we have to differentiate between hobbyists and those whose activities reach the level of trade or business. Typically, royalties received by taxpayers who are active in that business are taxed on a Schedule C, while royalties accrued by taxpayers who never were, or are no longer, active in that business are taxed on a Schedule E or as ordinary income.

Let's say Charlie buys an NFT from an artist, Dana, and the licensing rights are split between the two of them. Dana's income from those royalties would probably follow the tax treatment of the sale of the original asset; if Dana is a hobbyist, the royalties would not be considered active income. If, however, Dana is active in the trade or business of creating this type of asset, the royalties should be reported on the Schedule C, subject to self-employment tax.

Charlie is also earning royalties from licensing the NFT. Is Charlie active in the business of licensing? If so, this may be Schedule C income. If not, it is likely royalty income on Schedule E.

Having said all that, let me make it clear that the IRS has issued ZERO guidance on NFTs. I'm making recommendations based on how I think the taxation will go, but the IRS has been known to surprise us.

If you are reporting an NFT transaction on a tax return, and there is any doubt at all as to whether or not the treatment is correct, it would be a good idea to include Form 8275, *Disclosure Statement*, explaining what you're doing.

16

MMORPGs

You'll recall that way back in May 2013, the Government Accountability Office wrote a report to the Committee on Finance, U.S. Senate, called *Virtual Economies and Currencies: Additional IRS Guidance Could Reduce Tax Compliance Risks.* I provided it for you in Part I of this book.

The report has proven, again and again, to be spot-on in terms of predicting tax issues on the horizon. Not only did it predict the rise of virtual currency, but it also called out the issue of virtual economies created by online role-playing games.

The report first states, "There are no legal definitions for a virtual economy or currency, but generally, a virtual economy is comprised by the economic activities among a community of entities that interact within a virtual setting, such as an online, multi-user game."

The report discussed MMORPGs (massively multi-player online role-playing games) with closed-flow economies, open-flow economies and hybrid economies. In a closed-flow economy, virtual goods and services can be traded in-game, but no opportunity exists to trade such assets for dollars. In an open-flow economy, dollars can purchase in-game assets and in-game assets can be sold for dollars. In a hybrid economy, dollars can purchase in-game assets, but in-game assets cannot be sold for dollars.

What the report could not predict was the birth of the NFT. Through the medium of the NFT, assets that previously could not be sold in-game for dollars, now can indeed be sold for dollars, with ownership transferred via an NFT platform. Thus, increasingly, participation in online games can create taxable events. Some of the big games in that space are CryptoKitties, Spells of Genesis, Beyond the Void, Privateers Life and Worldopoly.

CryptoKitties centers around the collection and breeding of virtual cats, called Kitties. Each Kitty is unique. The game has a total of 4 billion possible Kitties, some rarer than others. There is no in-game store, but outside the game, these digital Kitties have been bought and sold, some for over $100,000. The game runs on the Ethereum blockchain, so you participate using ETH currency. The game is touted as a great way to get introduced to the world of blockchain and cryptocurrencies.

Spells of Genesis, aka SoG, is akin to Magic: The Gathering cards, but these cards are stored on the blockchain rather than being an actual physical card.

The cards are used in battle, with elements like health, speed and spells. This game uses the Bitcoin blockchain, so you need Bitcoin to play the game. Again, there is no in-game store, but assets can be bought and sold outside the game.

Beyond the Void offers players an online interstellar battle arena. In-game spaceships and other items are purchased via ETH and are registered on the blockchain. These assets can easily be bought and sold outside the game, though the developers have also created an online shop.

Privateers Life attempts to take the idea a step further and create an in-game economy that mirrors a real-life economy. Goods cannot appear out of the void; they have to be manufactured, harvested or mined from in-game materials. These goods can then be sold for cryptotokens. There's an in-game store to encourage buying and selling, with the developers taking a cut of all sales.

Worldopoly runs on the Ethereum blockchain. It allows players to buy and sell streets and buildings, erect hotels, rent out shopfronts, raid or burn competitors' buildings. (Note that the idea is to re-create real life as accurately as possible.)

Are there tax issues for these gamers? Yes, and lots of them. Any time a taxpayer gets involved in one of these games, they're using cryptocurrency to buy in, so right off the bat we've got a sale of, typically, Bitcoin or ETH. If all the player does, after that initial purchase, is stay within the game and not purchase any additional assets, there are no further tax events.

However, a good number of these gamers buy additional assets — again, using cryptocurrency — and then may buy and sell assets via an in-game store, or outside the game using an NFT platform. Tracking the basis of sold assets may prove complex, since the gamer may not be tracking how much it cost to create that in-game asset. If a taxpayer sells a Kitty from CryptoKitties online, what did it cost that taxpayer to create that Kitty? Have they tracked how much Ethereum they put into that game? And can they segregate how much of that Ethereum was directly related to the creation of this particular Kitty? Again, it's not clear that the new reporting requirements will apply to NFT platforms, so tax preparers will have to figure all this out on their own.

This sort of tracking may be difficult; but, as we well know, just because something's hard to track doesn't mean that it isn't taxable. It may be that tracking the basis of in-game assets will be the next new multimillion dollar app.

Part V

UPCOMING LEGISLATION

1
The Virtual Currency Tax Fairness Act

THERE'S LEGISLATION IN THE WINGS for virtual currency taxpayers.

The Virtual Currency Tax Fairness Act, introduced on July 26, 2022, is fairly straightforward. Its goal is to allow taxpayers to use cryptocurrencies for everyday transactions. As you now know, when someone swipes their Bitcoin debit card for a cup of coffee, a taxable transaction has taken place. And that might well make you decide to reach for a different debit card to buy that cup of joe.

But this act would keep such transactions off the tax return by instituting a $200 de minimis rule when using cryptocurrency to purchase goods and services. That $200 would be indexed for inflation.

2

Responsible Financial Innovation Act

THE RESPONSIBLE FINANCIAL INNOVATION ACT is a dense and far-reaching proposal that would make digital assets part of the overall U.S. financial system. It's a 69-page proposal, with eight titles and 54 sections, covering a wide variety of issues including taxes, securities, commodities, consumer protection, payments and stablecoins, banking laws, interagency coordination and further agency research.

According to one of its proponents, the objective of the bill is to "generate more flexibility, innovation, consumer protections, and transparency while providing more certainty and clarity to the growing digital assets industry."

Here's a fairly detailed summary, broken down by the eight titles.

Title 1 — Definitions

As of now, there are no universally accepted definitions for most digital industry terms. This bill would lock in definitions, namely:

- **"digital asset"** — (a) a natively electronic asset that (i) confers economic, proprietary, or access rights or powers and (ii) is recorded using cryptographically secured distributed ledger technology, or any similar analogue; and (b) includes (i) virtual currency and ancillary assets, (ii) payment stablecoins, and (iii) other securities and commodities.

- **"digital asset intermediary"** — (a) a person who holds a license, registration, or other similar authorization that may conduct market activities relating to digital assets, or a person who is required by law to hold such a license, registration or other similar authorization; and (b) includes a person who holds a license, registration, or other similar authorization under state or federal law that issues a payment stablecoin, or a person who is required by law to hold such a license, registration or other similar authorization; and (c) does not include a depository institution.

- **"distributed ledger technology"** — technology that enables the operation and use of a ledger that: (a) is shared across a set of distributed nodes that participate in a network and store a complete or partial replica of the ledger; (b) is synchronized between the nodes; (c) has data appended to the ledger by following the specified consensus mechanism of the ledger; (d) may be accessible to anyone or restricted to a subset of participants; and (e) may require participants to have authorizations to perform certain actions or require no authorization.

- **"payment stablecoin"** — a digital asset that is: (a) redeemable, on demand, on a one-to-one basis for instruments denominated in U.S. dollars and defined as legal tender or for instruments defined as legal tender under the laws of a foreign country (excluding digital assets defined as legal tender under the laws of a foreign country); (b) issued by a business entity; (c) accompanied by a statement from the issuer that the asset is redeemable from the issuer or another person; (d) backed by one or more financial assets (excluding other digital assets); and (e) intended to be used as a medium of exchange.

- **"smart contract"** — (a) (i) computer code deployed to a distributed ledger technology network that executes an instruction based on the occurrence or nonoccurrence of specified conditions; or (ii) any similar analogue; and (b) may include taking possession or control of a digital asset and transferring the asset or issuing executable instructions for these actions.

- **"virtual currency"** — (a) a digital asset that: (i) is used primarily as a medium of exchange, unit of account, store of value, or any combination of such functions; (ii) is not legal tender; and (iii) does not derive value from or is backed by an underlying financial asset (except other digital assets); and (b) includes a digital asset that is accompanied by a statement from the issuer that a denominated or pegged value will be maintained and be available upon redemption from the issuer or other identified person, based solely on a smart contract.

Title II — Taxation of Digital Assets

Certain tax benefits would be provided, namely:

- **Trading Safe Harbor for Non-US Persons (Sec. 203)** — safe harbors that apply to non-U.S. persons who use a U.S. institution for securities and commodities trading activity would, under certain conditions, extend to digital asset trading.

- **Decentralized Autonomous Organizations (Sec. 204)** — decentralized autonomous organizations (DAOs)[1] would be considered business entities for purposes of the tax code and would need to be properly incorporated or organized under the laws of a jurisdiction.

- **Digital Asset Lending Agreements (Sec. 205)** — digital asset lending transactions would not typically be taxable events, much like lending transactions related to securities.

- **Digital Asset Mining and Staking (Sec. 208)** — digital assets obtained through mining or staking activities would not be counted towards gross income until the "disposition" of those assets.

Title III — Securities Innovation

Under this bill, most digital currencies would be considered commodities, not securities. These currencies would be regulated by the Commodity Futures Trading Commission (CFTC), not the Securities and Exchange Commission (SEC).

A clear standard is proposed as to when a digital asset would be considered a commodity rather than a security. This section also discusses "ancillary assets," which are not things most of us need to worry about.

Note, though, that traders in cryptocurrencies regarded as either commodities or securities would be able to make a mark-to-market election.

Title IV — Responsible Commodities Innovation

This title further outlines what arrangements would fall under the SEC rather than the CFTC. In addition, the bill would:

- outline the restrictions under which futures commission merchants can conduct trading activities and use a customer's digital assets;

- provide a robust framework for digital asset exchanges to register with the CFTC and conduct trading activities;

- define registered digital asset exchanges as 'financial institutions' under the Bank Secrecy Act;

- afford digital assets similar treatment as commodities in bankruptcy and formulates other aspects of the treatment of digital assets in bankruptcy;

- determine that a payment stablecoin issued by a bank or credit union is neither a commodity nor a security; and

- enable the CFTC to impose a small user fee on digital asset exchanges to offset agency costs.

(We just can't seem to get away from these fees.)

Title V — Responsible Consumer Protection

A provider of digital asset services would be required to give customers certain information to help that customer make an informed decision. Particularly:

- notice of "material source code version changes relating to digital assets," prior to implementing the updates (with an exception for emergencies);

- whether and how customer digital assets are segregated from other customer assets;

- how the customer's assets would be treated in bankruptcy or insolvency, and the risks of loss;

- how long and in what manner the provider must return the customer's digital assets upon request;

- applicable fees; and

- the provider's dispute resolution process.

Title VI — Responsible Payment Innovation

This section relates directly to the crypto crash in the summer of 2022, in which a downward spiral in the value of digital currencies was prompted by the devaluing of a certain stablecoin. This bill hopes to prevent a recurrence by:

- requiring issuers to maintain "high-quality liquid assets" worth 100% of all outstanding stablecoins;

- imposing monthly disclosure requirements to describe the assets backing the stablecoins and their value;

- requiring issuers to have the ability to redeem any outstanding stablecoins at par value;

- instituting a detailed procedure for banks and credit unions to issue their own stablecoins;

- creating tailored holding company supervision for banks and credit unions exclusively engaged in issuing stablecoins; and

- establishing an "Innovation Laboratory" within FinCEN to study developments in financial technology, organize pilot projects and engage in dialogue with financial companies, and make legislative recommendations in order to maximize the supervision of financial technology.

Title VII — Responsible Banking Innovation

This bill would require the Board of Governors of the Federal Reserve to conduct a study discussing how distributed ledger technology can reduce risks for depository institutions. The Federal Reserve would also be responsible for issuing routing transit numbers to depository institutions. Any depository institution with a state charter, whether federal insured and supervised or not, would be eligible for an account at a Federal Reserve bank.

In order to prevent federal banking agencies from delaying these applications, this bill requires adherence to a one-year review period. Further, the prohibits federal banking agencies from using reputation risk in rating a depository institution. The federal banking agencies would instead need to provide adequate justifications for terminating a specific customer account.

Title VIII — Responsible Interagency Coordination

The last title of the bill requires:

- federal financial regulators to provide customized interpretive guidance within six months of a request;

- the Federal Energy Regulatory Commission, along with the CFTC and SEC, to analyze the energy consumption in the digital asset market;

- the CTFC and the SEC to study self-regulation in the digital asset markets and advance a proposal for the establishment of registered digital asset associations; and

- the CFTC and the SEC to develop cybersecurity guidance for digital asset intermediaries, on topics such as security operations, risk identification and reduction, and money laundering.

All in all, what we're seeing here is a call to action to bring digital assets under the umbrella of the federal government. It hasn't passed, and it might not.

Part VI
TAX MATTERS

1

Audits

THE IRS REQUIRES THAT ALL income, including virtual currency income and gains upon sale, be reported on the tax return for the year in which the income was received. The IRS further expects that documentation supporting the numbers on the tax return will be available for review upon request.

That said, it's been almost pathetically easy to get away with not paying taxes on income derived from virtual currency. This fact isn't lost on the IRS. The Service is starting to get very interested in taxpayers who earn/utilize/spend/invest in virtual currency.

Be aware that it's truly just a matter of time until the legal tangles are untangled, and the IRS gets its hands on a whole lot of data that will affect a whole lot of people. When that happens, those people are going to do a whole lot of scrambling to amend a whole lot of tax returns.

My advice is to accept the inevitable and start reporting your income immediately. If you don't understand how to do this yourself, get help. "I didn't understand" is not, has never been, and will never be something the IRS is interested in hearing.

Remember that the IRS guidance issued in 2014 was retroactive. If you had virtual currency income at any point, before or after 2014, and you didn't report it, it would be a good idea to amend those returns.

Under normal circumstances, the IRS has only three years to audit you; but there are special cases that can extend that time period. If you omitted more than 25% of your income, those three years become six years. And if you have committed tax fraud, there is no time limit. Read that again: NO TIME LIMIT. You'll be hiding under the bed for the rest of your life.

Don't count on the much-vaunted anonymity of virtual currency. While it may be possible for some very savvy trader to remain anonymous, this isn't an option for the average user of virtual currency who utilizes an exchange. Your identity is tied to your account by virtue of email contact and bank or credit card information. Once the IRS can identify a virtual currency account as belonging to an individual, they can extract every transaction from the blockchain.

Further, IRS activities such as Operation Hidden Treasure and the John Doe Summons to Circle and Kraken mean that tax evaders will eventually be found.

Your failure to report all your income can lead to nasty accuracy-related penalties... or worse. If the IRS decides that you've willfully engaged in tax fraud, it could decide that your case should be handled by the Criminal Investigation branch of the Service. It is not impossible for a careless virtual currency user to face felony tax evasion charges and a federal prison sentence.

Be aware that if your past virtual currency dealings create the potential for criminal charges, you need to speak with a tax attorney, not an Enrolled Agent or CPA. Only an actual attorney enjoys attorney-client privilege. Unless hired by a tax attorney under a Kovel agreement, an Enrolled Agent or CPA can be subpoenaed by the IRS and become a witness against you.

2

Best Practices for Virtual Currency Taxpayers

I OFFER THE FOLLOWING LIST of "Best Practices" for virtual currency users and investors who would like to avoid problems with the IRS.

1. Given the severity of the possible consequences, getting professional help really is the sensible choice. Don't rely on the nonsense that's passed around on crypto blogs. Find a tax preparer who has experience working with virtual currency taxation and get on their client list. The best time to do this is not — repeat, NOT — during tax season. (We're kind of busy then.)

2. Make sure you know the basis of all virtual currency you own. Document how you arrived at that basis. Use that basis moving forward. This isn't perfect, but it's better than

trying to figure it out years from now during a high-pressure audit.

3. If you can't maintain your own spread-sheets, stay with exchanges supported by the conversion platform of your choice. We don't know for certain if the IRS will accept the conclusions drawn by this type of software, but you'll at least be demonstrat-ing that you tried your best to report your income correctly.

4. Print out statements regularly; otherwise, if your exchange shuts down or your computer gets stolen, you'll have proof of NOTHING. If you don't like paper, then scan the report into a safe drive and then shred the paper. Document, document, document. If you can't document it, don't do it.

5. Separate your investment accounts from your personal use accounts. This makes it more likely that the IRS will allow you to take a loss on the investment account.

6. Recognize that tax law for virtual currency is in its infancy. We're all doing our best with very limited information. No one can predict the future of tax law — not even a highly trained and extremely intelligent Enrolled Agent.

3
Best Practices for Tax Preparers

OK, FELLOW TAX PREPARERS, THIS is for you.

1. Include the current crypto question in your standard engagement letter. Don't assume that someone isn't the virtual currency "type." You may be surprised to discover how many of your clients are dabbling in virtual currency.

2. Create an additional engagement letter for your virtual currency clients to sign. The engagement letter should inform the client that virtual currency tax law is in its infancy and subject to change and that the client is responsible for the accuracy of the data they provide. The engagement letter should also specifically ask what activities the client was engaged in: earning, investing, trading,

gifting, was a 1099K received, etc. You can find a suggested engagement letter under "Resources."

3. Utilize a special crypto questionnaire to have your clients reveal exactly what activities they've engaged in. This protects you in the event that client later comes back and suggests that you didn't put all her activities on her tax return. You'll find a suggested questionnaire under "Resources."

4. Spend some time with the client to make sure she understands her tax obligations relative to virtual currency. As has been mentioned, there is a lot of false information out in the blogs.

5. Unless you are comfortable with the client's level of expertise in preparing the data himself or herself, have the client utilize a software platform that creates a summary (Form 8949 or .csv file) for you to use in preparing the return.

6. If your client has inherited any virtual currency during the tax year, make sure she documents its fair market value ASAP.

7. Remember that it is still incumbent upon you, if you are a Circular 230 practitioner, to ask questions. How did the client obtain this information? Were all files exported to the software? Etc.

8. Don't take risks for the client; your license is more important than saving the client a bit of tax money. (And you know that client will throw you under the bus in a heartbeat if the IRS starts asking questions.)

9. Stay educated on crypto; take classes from tax professionals who are specializing in it. Cryptocurrency is not going away. Unless you plan to retire real soon, you're going to have to bite the virtual bullet and get comfortable with cryptocurrency taxation. You may wish to join this Facebook group: Crypto Tax Pros United States. It's open only to tax professionals, so provide your credentials when you ask to join. This Facebook Group was set up to allow tax pros to communicate with one another when they're confused about a crypto tax situation.

Resources

Here's the wording I suggest for your engagement letter. I'm not an attorney, remember, so I don't guarantee how this will stand up in a court of law.

Cryptocurrency and DeFi Engagement Letter

We will perform the following services in connection with your cryptocurrency and centralized finance transactions:

1. Prepare the tax return using tax guidance issued by the IRS.

2. Utilize general tax principles and our best professional judgment in those areas where IRS guidance is silent.

3. Explain options if they exist.

You understand that virtual currency tax law is in its infancy. We assume no liability for tax, penalties or interest that occur as a result of changes to, or clarification of, the taxation of cryptocurrency and other decentralized finance transactions.

You also understand that you are solely responsible for providing correct information with regard to your income, fair market values, sale information, basis documentation, and any other information required to correctly prepare your tax return. We are unable to sift through raw data. If you don't maintain your own records, plan to use an online software platform to calculate gains and losses.

If you are still our client when the IRS issues clarification of virtual currency and decentralized finance tax law, we will inform you if we believe prior year returns prepared by us should be amended in the light of new information.

If this letter is in agreement with your understanding of our engagement, please sign below.

_____   _____
Taxpayer   Date

Here's the questionnaire I recommend for crypto clients; format yours in a Yes/No manner:

Cryptocurrency Questionnaire

1. I earned cryptocurrency through mining or by working for others.

2. I sold, traded or spent cryptocurrency.

3. I track gains and losses on my own.

4. I use an online app to track gains and losses.

5. I gave or loaned cryptocurrency.

6. I inherited or received cryptocurrency as a gift, an inheritance, or in some other manner.

7. I lost cryptocurrency in some manner other than a sale.

8. I received forked/airdropped cryptocurrency.

   FMV of forked/airdropped currency $_____

9. I held cryptocurrency in a foreign exchange.

10. I purchased assets in an initial coin/initial exchange/initial DeFi/initial token or similar offering.

11. I received interest, dividends, node rewards or similar type of income from cryptocurrency activities.

    Value of interest/dividends/node rewards $\$$_____

12. I participated in cryptocurrency, NFTs, or other types of blockchain activities in a manner not mentioned above.

Disclaimer

I said it before, but for those who weren't listening: *this booklet is intended as a general commentary on virtual currency taxation. It is not intended to represent tax law, nor is it intended to apply to any reader's particular tax situation. It is no substitute for the advice of your own tax professional. As an IRS Circular 230 practitioner, I have no responsibility for any positions you take on your tax return, unless I have prepared and signed that tax return. For a detailed analysis of your tax situation, please consult your tax advisor.*

Remember that the tax law which applies to virtual currency is in its early stages, and future alterations are likely. As with virtual currency in general, you proceed at your own risk. The author owns some virtual currency, but has no vested interest in any particular platform, currency, or corporation.

If you're dying to reach me with questions or complaints, you can email me at amy@amywall.com. Note, please, that I am not taking on clients or preparing tax returns at this time, but I'm always interested in hearing about tax situations involving cryptocurrency.

www.ingramcontent.com/pod-product-compliance
Lightning Source LLC
Chambersburg PA
CBHW061208220326
41597CB00015BA/1559